The High Way
of Forgiveness

The High Way

of Forgiveness

by

Gwen Shaw

Engeltal Press
P.O. Box 447
Jasper, ARK 72641 U.S.A.
Telephone: +1 (870) 446-2665
www.EngeltalPress.com

All scripture references are from the King James Version
unless otherwise specified.

The Message (MSG) Copyright © 1993, 1994, 1995, 1996, 2000, 2001, 2002 by
Eugene H. Peterson. Used by permission of NavPress Publishing Group.

Amplified Bible (AMP) Copyright © 1954, 1958, 1962, 1964, 1965, 1987 by
The Lockman Foundation. Used with permission.

ISBN 978-0-9846355-2-8

Cover painting: "Love Remembers" by Rebekah Laue
www.stretcherbearers.com

Printed in the United States of America

Dedication and Tribute

to

Lt. Col. James von Doornum Shaw

The Shaws, 2005

When you came into my life, God gave me everything I ever dreamed—and more.

God gave me a man to match my mountains— and they were many, and they were high. There was nothing that the two of us feared when we were together. We laughed together, cried together, loved the same music, the same places. We enjoyed a challenge, no matter how dangerous. More than once you "rescued" me out of trouble, and that was at a risk to your own self. I never saw you flinch once when we flew through icy storms. When I knew we were in danger as the ice hit the windows of our small plane, I would look at your face, and all I saw was courage and faith; and my heart would take courage from you. You were my hero-and you still are. You were in my past, and you are in my future. Love is forever.

∽∾

Five years ago, on March 5, 2007, Jim closed his eyes here on earth. The next person he saw was Jesus. It happened so fast. If we could only realize that Heaven is only a heartbeat away! I wonder if we would be so careless with the gift of time if we knew how many days we had left.

The amazing thing is, the day I finished writing this book, I was reminded that it was what would have been Jim's 93rd birthday, June 5, 2012. I know that if he were here, he would be moved to tears by this message from the Lord. I pray that it will be life-changing for all who read it.

Table of Contents

Introduction

Beloved Reader,

As the coming of the Lord draws nigh, we who have searched the scriptures know that He is coming for a Bride who has made herself ready. It is therefore our duty to search our hearts to make sure that we will be ready for His coming.

One of the most important things is that there is no unforgiveness in our hearts. We have all experienced reasons to be hurt and offended by things that have happened to us in our lifetime. Often those whom we love the most have hurt us the most. So it's hard to keep your heart pure and free from angers and unforgiveness. But the Bride of Christ must be arrayed in white raiment of linen, which is the righteousness of the saints.

Therefore let us be very honest with ourselves and let the Holy Spirit search our hearts for anything that would keep us from that glorious company of the firstborn, even the Bridal Company.

I have not written this book without doing a lot of soul-searching myself. If you feel convicted of anything as you read it, know that I have been convicted myself as I have written it. May we all become as little children, for of such is the Kingdom of God.

Your sister and mother in Christ,

Sister Gwen

The High Way
of Forgiveness

Forgiveness, the Key to Heaven

I feel it is only right that I begin this message with the Lord's Prayer as it is recorded in Matthew 6:9-13.

"After this manner therefore pray ye: Our Father which art in heaven, Hallowed be thy name. [10] Thy kingdom come. Thy will be done in earth, as it is in heaven. [11] Give us this day our daily bread. [12] And forgive us our debts, as we forgive our debtors. [13] And lead us not into temptation, but deliver us from evil: For thine is the kingdom, and the power, and the glory, for ever. Amen."

This is the prayer we learned from our childhood. I remember praying this beautiful prayer every morning at the beginning of our school day when I was a student in a little country schoolhouse in

Saskatchewan, Canada. It is a short prayer, but it covers every vital area of our lives.

In the heart of this prayer lies the key to Heaven. It is FORGIVE. First, we ask God to forgive us our trespasses and sins; but the key lies in the weighty words, *"As we forgive our debtors."* Jesus, who taught us this prayer, clarified that my ability to be forgiven for my misdeeds was dependent upon my willingness to forgive everyone who had hurt me in any way. This is something we are often not willing to do. We want to hang on to our offences and hurts, not realizing that we are harming ourselves more than the one who has offended us. Some of us carry years of baggage. We are so weighed down with "overload" that we are miserable, sick, crippled, and mentally handicapped. We become bitter, angry, unlovable, and hard-to-live-with people.

According to the original Greek, the words "as we forgive" would be better translated, "as we have forgiven." Richard Wurmbrand, the Romanian pastor who suffered vicious torture in prison for preaching about Jesus, commented on this scripture, that it was very helpful for them to forgive their persecutors before they ever even hurt them.

There is a mystery about verse twelve (12); the word commonly used in the Greek versions of the

New Testament for "have forgiven" is "aphekamen" which means "to send off or send away; to let go or dismiss." Relating to sin, it means that God will send away our sins as far as the east is from the west. When relating to forgiveness, it has the sense of "sending away from yourself, the sins that others have committed toward you."

The Amplified Bible renders Matthew 6:12 this way: *"And forgive us our debts, as we also have forgiven (left, remitted, and let go of the debts, and have given up resentment against) our debtors."*

When I worked behind the Iron Curtain of East Europe, I met many saints who had suffered great tribulation under Communism. I, myself, have experienced the love of God for my interrogators when I was arrested and forced to strip myself twice. It is a purely divine, supernatural experience to be able to love your persecutors. We have to prepare our hearts to live through the persecution that is coming; yea, and it has already begun.

We never have had so many people turning violent. The world is seeing more and more of this kind of people. They walk into a restaurant and begin shooting and killing innocent people against whom they do not even have a grudge. Soon they have a grudge against the whole world; they blow up planes, and buildings, and set forests and cities on fire. They instigate wars: killing and maiming hundreds of thousands. Adolph Hitler had so much hatred and anger that he started a world war that ultimately caused the death of six hundred million lives.

Anger is the father of hatred. So we must be careful to weed out of the garden of our hearts any anger we may have towards anyone—even though we may feel that we are justified in being angry. We must rid our hearts at all times from any seeds the devil may try to sow in our spirits because it will mar us and warp our entire lives.

George and Mary

I had an uncle whose name was George. He was married to a beautiful woman called Mary, whom he loved dearly. They lived in Kansas. I still have in my possession some of their love letters they wrote to each other. They had one adopted son. One day, Uncle George was coming home from work, looking forward to being home with his wife. It must have been in the winter, because the lights were on in the houses. As he passed by the house of a minister of a church, he looked in the window and was shocked to see his wife sitting on the lap of the preacher who lived in that house. Immediately, his heart was filled with terrible anger against his wife, the preacher, God, all religion, and the whole world. Their marriage ended in divorce, and his was a life of anger and bitterness. He began a life of wandering; no one knew where he was for a long time. When he finally returned to his own family in Canada, he was still angry and miserable. He was a chain smoker that left him with lung trouble—coughing, spitting, and cursing. His brother's wives refused to let him live with them. Only my father and mother took him in. He lived with us for many years. He was a man of many gifts—builder, cabinet maker, and inventor. I used to spend hours talking with him. He admired Adolph Hitler. He would listen to him on shortwave radio, and say, "Canada needs a man like him." That was before World War II broke out. Until then, many were deceived by Hitler through his powerful orations and promises of bringing into Germany, and the world, the Thousand Year Kingdom. But, like most politicians—you do not know the man until he comes into office.

Be careful of the intimate relationships you make. Don't be deceived by outward appearances. Judas Iscariot was the "church treasurer" and one of the twelve honourable apostles until Satan entered into him (John 13:27).

Many poor souls have found out they have married "the devil" on their wedding night. I heard of one man who said, "I didn't marry the devil, but I married his sister!"

If you are one of these unfortunate victims of having made a wrong decision in marriage, or even living in a common-law relationship, and are suffering because of it, you have an opportunity to walk in the words the Master spoke to Peter when he asked Him, *"How oft shall my brother sin against me, and I forgive him? till seven times? [22] Jesus saith unto him, I say not unto thee, until seven times: but, Until seventy times seven"* (Matthew 18:21-22).

Our God is a God of forgiveness. My father prayed much for his brother. I loved him, and prayed for him also. When I was born again the whole household was turned upside down. My uncle and I had an altercation, which resulted in my going into my bedroom to pray for him; and it was while praying and travailing for him (a first-time experience for me), I was filled with the Holy Spirit, and prayed with other tongues, like the disciples did on the Day of Pentecost (Acts 2:1-4). I believe I will see Uncle George in Heaven. Perhaps, even his wife, Mary, will be there too! We cannot limit the Saviour's love, because we know that *"He is not willing that any should perish, but that all should come to repentance"* (2 Peter 3:9).

Sins Forgiven Still Leave Their Consequences

Never let the devil accuse you that you have to go to Hell; that you cannot be forgiven because you have sinned too many times. If Jesus told us that we must be willing to forgive seventy times seven (Matthew 18:21), we can be sure that unlimited love can forgive unlimited times, if we come to God with a contrite heart and sincerely ask His forgiveness. But we must also remember, when Jesus healed the man at the Pool of Bethesda, who had been crippled for thirty-eight years, He warned him, *"Behold, thou art made whole: sin no more, lest a worse thing come unto thee"* (John 5:14b). Sin has its consequences, even though we are forgiven. There is always a price to pay.

Germany paid a terrible price for following Hitler. Her great and beautiful cities were bombed into ruinous heaps of rubble. Millions of their sons and fathers died on the battlefield. Of the 285,100 German soldiers sent into the Soviet Union, only 49,000 evacuated, 130,000 were slaughtered, and 91,000 were taken prisoner, of which only 6,000 returned to Germany after their defeat at

Stalingrad. When I was ministering in Germany, many women told me that they had lost their husbands in Russia. Many waited in vain for many years, hoping they would some day come home. Every M.I.A. (missing in action) is a tragedy. But, when most of the remnant of Germany repented and wept before God, He forgave Germany and restored her with much help from America. Today she is one of the most prosperous nations in Europe. I have spent much time in Germany. I was even enabled, by the help of the Holy Spirit, to minister in the German language. It is a nation close to my heart. But it is a nation that needs a mighty Holy Ghost revival, a true visitation of God. Pray for Germany! May she walk humbly before God.

When King David repented for his sin of committing adultery with Bathsheba and the death of her husband in battle, he still had to pay a costly price, a price he had demanded a guilty man should pay when Nathan the prophet, told him a story. David demanded the man should pay back *"four times over"* for his evil deeds, not realizing he was passing judgment on himself (2 Samuel 12:6). And that is what happened to David: First, his unnamed son by Bathsheba died, and then three of his adult sons: Amnon, Absalom, and Adonijah died as a result of family angers.

To Be Able to Forgive Is
One of the Greatest Miracles

To be able to forgive someone who has deeply hurt and wounded you is one of the greatest miracles we can experience. That is because our wounds are much deeper than the skin. They affect the three-part man—body, soul, and spirit. If someone speaks unkind words to you, it will not cause your body to bleed, but it will affect your mind, it will bring torment to your soul, and could even send your never-dying soul to Hell. Day after day you will think about it and talk about it, until it robs you of all your peace of mind. You become a prisoner, living in a cell of unforgiveness. You look for people who will become sympathetic to your cause. You may even pay big money to a lawyer to fight for "your rights."

Paul dealt with this problem in the Church at Corinth in 1 Corinthians 6:1-10: *"Dare any of you, having a matter against another, go to law before the unjust, and not before the saints? [2] Do ye not know that the saints shall judge the world? And if the world shall be judged by you, are ye unworthy to judge the smallest matters? [3] Know ye not that we shall judge angels? How much more things that pertain to this life? [4] If then ye have judgments of things pertaining to this life, set them to judge who are least esteemed in the church. [5] I speak to your shame. Is it so, that there is not a wise man among you? no, not one that shall be able to judge between his brethren? [6] But brother goeth to law with brother, and that before the unbelievers. [7] Now therefore there is utterly a fault among you, because ye go to law one with another. Why do ye not rather take wrong? why do ye not rather suffer yourselves to be defrauded? [8] Nay, ye do wrong, and defraud, and that your brethren. [9] Know ye not that the unrighteous shall not inherit the kingdom of God? Be not deceived: neither fornicators, nor idolaters, nor adulterers, nor effeminate, nor abusers of themselves with mankind, [10] Nor thieves, nor covetous, nor drunkards, nor revilers, nor extortioners, shall inherit the kingdom of God."*

Jesus taught us to take the blame, even though we are innocent. Eternity will reveal the truth. Every sin will be settled at the Judgment Seat of Christ. He said *"Agree with thine adversary quickly, whiles thou art in the way with him; lest at any time the adversary deliver thee to the judge, and the judge deliver thee to the officer, and thou be cast into prison. [26] Verily I say unto thee, Thou shalt by no means come out thence, till thou hast paid the uttermost farthing"* (Matthew 5:25-26). If we go to war against our enemy, we will perish by the sword, but if we wear the armour of love, we will be protected.

I believe that to be able to forgive and to continue forgiving is the most beautiful way we can put on Christ. He forgave the people who crucified Him and then sat down to watch Him suffer, mocking Him, as He hung naked and in great agony on the cross. His first words were, *"Father forgive them; for they know not what they do"* (Luke 23:34).

Forgiving Angels

I have had many opportunities to forgive. No one can wound you as deeply as those who are close to your heart. For years, I struggled to forgive someone who had broken my heart. And then, one day I received a letter from that one, asking forgiveness; immediately I was able to forgive. It was so easy. Then the Holy Spirit showed me that an "angel of forgiveness" had accompanied the letter.

If you feel that you are going to go through some hard experiences, rejection, mockery, and maybe even physical suffering, determine in your heart ahead of time to forgive, and determine you will not hold a grudge in your heart. The angels will be there, waiting to help you.

Pray for your "thorn in the flesh." Immediately after Judas had agreed to betray Jesus, Jesus said, *"The Son of man goeth as it is written of him: but woe unto that man by whom the Son of man is betrayed! it had been good for that man if he had not been born"* (Matthew 26:24). It was while Jesus was eating the Passover Meal in the Upper Room that "Satan entered into Judas Iscariot" (John 13:27). You can afford to forgive your "thorn in the flesh" when you realize the judgment that awaits them for persecuting the Holy Ghost in you. Always remember it is not you they are persecuting, it is the Christ in you. You are helping Him carry the cross to Calvary.

The first sermon Jesus preached was The Sermon on the Mount; in it, He referred to persecution when He said, *"Blessed are they which are persecuted for righteousness' sake: for theirs is the kingdom of heaven. [11] Blessed are ye, when men shall revile you, and persecute you, and shall say all manner of evil against you falsely, for my sake. [12] Rejoice, and be exceeding glad: for great is your reward in heaven: for so persecuted they the prophets which were before you"* (Matthew 5:10-12).

The Dark Night of the Soul

Not only do good angels accompany letters, and gifts, evil spirits of condemnation and curses can accompany them also bringing sickness and depression, and even suicide. I know, because one day on the mission field I received a letter of accusation. It plunged me into a terrible feeling that God had left me. I was a lost soul—like Saul, and Esau, and Judas. I was living a lie. I wasn't really the holy, anointed missionary people thought I was. I might as well give up. As I stood on my little balcony sixteen storeys high, the thought came to me, "Why don't I just throw myself down, in one minute it will be over!"

For one week I suffered what Jesus suffered when, after hanging almost six hours in agony from the cross, He cried with a loud voice, saying, *"Eloi, Eloi, lama sabachthani?"* (*"My God, my God, why hast thou forsaken me?"*) (Mark 15:34).

It was now three o'clock in the afternoon. Until then He had not complained about the pain, but the agony of feeling forsaken by God was more than He could bear. This is called The Dark Night of the Soul. That is what I went through for about a week. I had no one I could share my heart with.

Then an anointed minister from Indonesia came to Hong Kong to preach in our churches. I had to interpret for him from English into Chinese. I felt like a Pharisee, standing there and interpreting. We had taken the boat to Macao for a series of meetings. My friend, Alice, was with us. She noticed something was wrong with me, but she didn't say anything until after the meeting that night. Then she asked me what was troubling me, so I told her my story. Bless her heart, she understood. She had gone through the same experience, and was able to speak the Word of God to me, and comfort me, assuring me of my salvation—not through my good works, but through the Precious Blood of Jesus.

If something is tormenting you, look around your house. Maybe there are some demonized articles you need to get rid of. Don't sell them to another poor soul. Burn them up. You may even hear demons cry out from the flames as they burn. But you will be free.

Forgiveness Is Life-Long

When we are enabled to forgive, it is a "forever" experience. This is because forgiveness is given to us by the Holy Spirit. When God forgives us of our sins, He promises to "remember them against us no more" (Hebrews 10:17). Oh, the wonderful comfort of Hebrews 8:12, *"For I will be merciful to their unrighteousness, and their sins and their iniquities will I remember no more!"*

When I Was a Prodigal Daughter

When I was seventeen years old, I ran away from home. My parents didn't know where I was, so they prayed. I was living in Toronto with my girlfriend. It was during World War II. Uncle George was still living with us. He was very angry, so he went to the police, but my parents refused to go; instead, they went to the Throne Room. After several months, Dad and Uncle George found out where I was working as a waitress in the heart of the city. I was standing in the restaurant kitchen when the door swung open, and in walked my dad! All I could see in his eyes was love. So I went to him, put my arms around his neck, and said, "Daddy, I am sorry!" He put his strong arms around me, and answered, "It's all right, Daughter. We won't talk about it." And he never did! Several months later I was saved. A month after that I was filled with the Holy Spirit, and after another month I was in Bible College. There always was a strong bond between my father and me.

It was my father's love for me that enabled him to forgive me for the pain I had given him and mother. Love is more powerful than all the pains we have suffered, and find so hard to forgive. *"The love of God is shed abroad in our hearts by the Holy Ghost"* (Romans 5:5). The more we allow the Holy Spirit to take over our lives, and live in us, the more we will be able to forgive those who painfully abuse us. This word for "love" is *agapé*—a love so great it can only describe the kind of love that flows from the heart of God. If we have this eternal *agapé* love in our heart, we are able to forgive eternally. It is impossible to truly forgive without supernatural, God-given, Holy Spirit-inspired love, *"because the love of God is shed abroad in our hearts by the Holy Ghost which is given unto us"* (Romans 5:5).

When you forgive, you have to stop holding a grudge. You won't be able to keep talking about it. You will be able to forget much of the painful past. I can remember crying, being broken-hearted, and wishing to die. But I can't remember why. This is the miracle of true forgiveness. Without true God-given *agapé* love, we are not able to forgive.

Remember how Jesus travailed and prayed in great agony on the night He was arrested in Gethsemane—He was comforted by one of the Heavenly Comforting Angels. The Comforting Angel worked together with the Forgiving Angel, so that when Judas, who had betrayed Him, arrived with the multitude to arrest Him, Jesus called him

—28—

"friend" (Matthew 26:50). He never stopped loving him. He knew how dreadful Judas' end would be. Jesus had foretold it while they were eating the Last Supper. It was then that He said, *"The Son of man indeed goeth, as it is written of him: but woe to that man by whom the Son of man is betrayed! good were it for that man if he had never been born."* (Mark 14:21).

While Jesus was hanging on the cross, the devil, having accomplished his evil deed through Judas, left him, for demons do not stay in a dying person. Judas, now filled with remorse, came to himself, and brought the betrayal money back to the chief priests and elders and said, *"'I have sinned in that I have betrayed the innocent blood.' And they said, 'What is that to us? See thou to that.' And he cast down the pieces of silver in the temple, and departed, and went and hanged himself"* (Matthew 27:4-5).

Five hundred years earlier the prophet Zechariah had prophesied these facts in Zechariah 11:12-13. He even foretold that the Potter's Field would be purchased with that blood money, which is exactly what happened (Matthew 27:9-10).

Jesus was not hanging alone; Judas was hanging also. Jesus hung for the sins of the world. Judas hung for his own sins. They were so great, so heavy, that the branch could not bear the weight, it broke, and he *"burst asunder in the midst, and all his bowels gushed out"* (Acts 1:18). He died a "double death." He is suffering in Hell today while you are reading this book.

Always Seek Forgiveness from Anyone Who Has Something Against You.

If you have grieved or injured any soul, ask them to forgive you, and then run to Jesus for forgiveness. And if you have been injured by anyone, forgive that person, even though they are not seeking for your forgiveness. You can't afford the price of unforgiveness. It will rob you of your peace of mind and soul, and can even bring sickness on your body.

Jesus said, *"Blessed are the meek: for they shall inherit the earth"* (Matthew 5:5). The word "meek" does not mean "weak." It can be interpreted as humble, or gentle. When you give a gentle answer to an angry man it can help to calm him down. *"A soft answer turneth away wrath, but grievous words stir up anger"* (Proverbs 15:1).

I remember one day when my husband Jim and I were having lunch with Richard and Sabina Wurmbrand. Both of them had spent many years in prison for the Lord Jesus in Romania. We were talking about the harsh and angry attitude of the people who were living behind the Iron Curtain. Brother Wurmbrand said, "We must be so careful not to take on their spirit when dealing with anyone—even buying a loaf of bread can make you angry when you are treated like a beggar, rather than a customer." I took that word to my heart. God's Word says in Psalm 18:35, *"Thy gentleness hath made me great."*

Don't Come to God with Unforgiveness in Your Heart

Jesus told us that we should not give God a gift without first making sure we have forgiven everyone. *"If thou bring thy gift to the altar, and there rememberest that thy brother hath ought against thee; Leave there thy gift before the altar, and go thy way; first be reconciled to thy brother, and then come and offer thy gift"* (Matthew 5:23-24).

Maybe your gift is money, worship, or some kind of ministry—it doesn't matter—make sure your heart is right with God and you have tried to live in peace with your fellowman.

Mark 11:25-26 says, *"And when ye stand praying, forgive, if ye have ought against any: that your Father also which is in heaven may forgive you your*

*trespasses. But if ye do not forgive, neither will your
Father which is in heaven forgive your trespasses.”*

Those are strong words of warning. It means
exactly what it says—that if I do not forgive others,
God cannot forgive me. I lay the condition of my
relationship with God by my relationship with
others. No matter what good works I may do, or
what gifts I may desire to give Him, my entire life,
now and tomorrow, depends on my willingness to
forgive others for the pain I have suffered from
them.

God spoke to my heart long ago and told me that
I can afford to be misunderstood for a little while,
because in Heaven all truth will be made open to
the eyes of man. I can wait that long—so can you.

Jesus taught us how to attempt to make peace
with people who have ought against us in Matthew
18:15-17, *“Moreover if thy brother shall trespass
against thee, go and tell him his fault between thee
and him alone: if he shall hear thee, thou hast gained
thy brother. But if he will not hear thee, then take
with thee one or two more, that in the mouth of two
or three witnesses every word may be established.
And if he shall neglect to hear them, tell it unto the
church: but if he neglect to hear the church, let him
be unto thee as an heathen man and a publican.”*

Do Not Take the Serpent to Your Bosom

There are some people with whom one cannot make peace. Proverbs 24:21 warns us, *"Meddle not with them that are given to change."*

I remember Rev. Wallace Heflin, Senior, warning his daughter, Ruth, and me one day as we were sitting in the camp dining room, "Girls, if you ever feel a kind of unseen veil come down between you and someone, take it as a warning from the Holy Spirit. He is trying to protect you from someone who could be your friend today, and your enemy tomorrow. Never ignore it, nor try to push it aside, thinking it is your imagination!" I believe this is what Jesus meant when He said, *"Let him be unto thee as an heathen man and a publican."* Love him, and if he has wronged you, forgive him, and leave him. Do not seek to have fellowship with him. Remember what the rabbi in *Fiddler on the Roof* said, "May God bless and keep the Tsar... far away from us!"

Satan has often destroyed wonderful people through the influence of a person he "plants" in their lives. It can be a weeping woman who comes to the pastor, telling him about how she is suffering from her husband. Or it could be a lonely, traveling evangelist or musician who is absent too long from his wife, or her husband, and the devil is ready to spring his trap. She may not be wicked, but soon a sympathetic demon unites them. The man or woman of God must never counsel anyone of the opposite gender alone. They must always have another woman or spiritual mother in the room. Even doctors do not see their patients without a nurse beside them.

Love Can Change a Hard and Hurting Heart

Recently, when I was spending some time in the hospital, I noticed how loving and gentle all the young nurses were. I asked them what had happened to the older, grouchy nurses, had they prayed them out? They giggled. Then near the end of my five-day stay, a nurse came in who was a model of the former rude and unkind nurses. I asked her how long she had been there. "Thirty years," she answered me. She was rude and unkind. When she walked out of the room I thought about it. I had to make a decision, would I treat her with the same attitude with which she treated me, or would I treat her with love? I decided the only way that was right: I would love her. The next time she came in the room (she was my nurse that day), I spoke kindly to her and complemented her on dedicating her life to the suffering people of the world, and told her she would be given a reward from God for all the good deeds she had done. Immediately, her attitude changed. When her day was finished, she came in to tell me goodbye—we were friends.

Always remember, *"A soft answer turneth away wrath: but grievous words stir up anger"* (Proverbs 15:1).

The Prodigal Son

One of my favourite Bible stories is Jesus' parable about the prodigal son in Luke 15:11-32. A father had two sons. One was hard-working and faithful, but the younger one was a "playboy." He wanted to be free, so he asked his father to give him his share of their legacy. After receiving it, he headed off to the big city. He was the new attraction. He lived first class, ate in the finest restaurants, drank with the alcoholics, and slept with the harlots until his money ran out. Famine came to the land; he had no profession nor expertise; the only thing he knew anything about was farming, so he couldn't find a job. Someone sent him out to his pig farm. Day after day, he slopped the pigs, looked at the pigs, and smelled the pigs, until he began to feel like one. Life was miserable. He was starving.

Then one day, he came to his senses, he decided to go back home to his father's farm, and be his hired servant. When he arrived, he found his father waiting for him with open arms. He gave his son a new robe, the family signet ring, and new shoes. Then he ordered a great welcome party with music and dancing. All because his son had humbled himself and asked for forgiveness.

Why is it so hard to say, "I am sorry; Forgive me"? Our pride can keep us locked out of Heaven. Don't let it happen to you. It is time to be a peacemaker. Jesus said, *"Blessed are the peacemakers: for they shall be called the children of God"* (Matthew 5:9).

The prodigal son confessed his wrong deed. It will make it easier for others to forgive you when you confess your faults. You are not perfect. You have made mistakes. Make an honest inventory of your own soul. Don't look for a scapegoat.

Let your confession not be only empty words; be honest with yourself, and speak from your heart. Be sincere. Only then will you be called the child of God.

When we read the genealogy of Jesus in Luke we read, *"...Seth, which was the son of Adam, which was the son of God."* We are his offspring—His descendents. We want to get back our inheritance, our legacy, which Adam and Eve lost through sin, and Jesus redeemed back for us. It is rightfully ours. But we must repent, confess our sins, and accept the gift of full salvation

The High Way of Forgiveness

through Jesus Christ, our Saviour: *"Christ in you, the hope of glory"* (Colossians 1:27).

My first official sermon that I preached was in Aurora, Ontario, in the little Pentecostal Assemblies of Canada church where I had rejected Jesus for so long, and everyone knew me. My message was "The Prodigal Son." Everyone rejoiced for the great miracle of transformation that had taken place in my life. You can read more about it in my biography, *Unconditional Surrender*, and see pictures of it on the DVD by the same name (see page 113).

Bob and Jenny

Some people have to be convinced to repent of their misdeeds through harsher persuasion—like Bob. Bob was the only child in a dysfunctional home where his father had been cruel to his mother. We all knew Bob, and liked him. He married Jenny, one of our church girls from a large Italian family. She had older brothers, and was their darling little sister. When Bob began treating her harshly like his father (who had been his example), even hurting her, he had not reckoned with her Italian brothers, for when they saw her bruises, they "paid Bob a visit." Before they left they warned him that if he ever again treated their sister like he had, they would visit him again, and the next visit would be worse than this

—37—

one. Needless to say, Bob took the warning, and he
and Jenny lived happily ever after. But where are
the family defenders today? Why do so many of us
have to suffer alone? Is there no brother who will
defend the hurt and abused woman?

The Greatness of God in You

God is great because He is more willing to forgive
than to punish. It hurts Him to see us suffer. When
my father whipped me (and I deserved it), he said,
"Daughter, this hurts me more than it hurts you!"
I saw him weeping. The Bible says that God *"is not
willing that any should perish, but that all should
come to repentance"* (2 Peter 3:9).

When you are more willing to forgive than
to punish the wrongdoer, you are revealing the
greatness of God that is in you. It shows true *agapé*
love. This is more than mortal love, it is divine love,
the "force" that created all things. You will not seek
to build your own little kingdom, but everything
you do will be for others.

How to Enable Yourself to Forgive

When Jesus was crucified, His first words were,
*"Father, forgive them; for they know not what they
do"* (Luke 23:34). He was more concerned for them
than he was for Himself. He had found them in

the spirit. He knew that most of them were good Jewish men, loving fathers, faithful to their wives, and observers of the Law. He knew they had been whipped into this frenzy of madness, just like Pilate knew that it was *"for envy they had delivered him up"* (Matthew 27:18). He also knew that the Roman soldiers were just following orders and had no idea Who He was due to their pagan upbringing.

Jealousy, alcohol, drugs, and demons can change a person. When you have trouble with someone, try to see them as God sees what they were meant to be. Have pity and mercy. It will be easier to forgive.

Be humble enough and honest with yourself to search your own heart and admit your own wrong-doing.

It wasn't always easy to live together with many missionaries in one house. I remember an incident that took place in Taiwan. We were missionaries from America, Canada, and England. The work was divided up among us, a week at a time. For one week one of the women was in charge of house cleaning, another was in charge of the cooking, etc. One day, I happened to hear the other women complain that I was a very poor house cleaner. I ran to my prayer closet, fell on my knees, and cried out to God, "Lord, did you hear what they said about me?" I opened my

Bible to find a Word to vindicate and comfort me. The first words my eyes fell on were Ecclesiastes 7:21-22 *"Also take no heed unto all words that are spoken; lest thou hear thy servant curse thee: For oftentimes also thine own heart knoweth that thou thyself likewise hast cursed others."*

I stood up, picked up the duster, the mop, and went to work, a humbler and wiser woman—and also a better housekeeper.

The Holy Ghost helped me to forgive when I went to God for help. He helped me to be a better homemaker, and a better woman of God.

You Must Forgive Yourself

When we look back at our past, we all can remember foolish mistakes we have made, even from our youth. Some of the things I regret the most were words or deeds which I thought would be funny. We have to learn to keep a watch over our tongues.

There never was a day my father didn't pray in our morning family devotions, *"Set a watch, O Lord, before my mouth; keep the door of my lips"* (Psalm 141:3). I used to wonder why he prayed that prayer because he was a man of few words. He never spoke evil against anyone, neither did he repeat a bit of bad information about anyone, even to my mother.

When you and I look back at our past, we will wish we had not done some of the things we did, but we must take our sins to the cross and leave them there. Remember He died and shed His blood to wash them away forever. He has forgiven you. Now, you must forgive yourself.

God can work something good out of our sins. One of King David's greatest sins was counting Israel. This was a direct breaking of the commandment of the Lord. A plague broke out that took the lives of seventy thousand men. It was probably the same destroying angel that passed through Egypt on Passover Night. When the angel arrived at Jerusalem, God stopped him at the threshing floor of Araunah, the Jebusite. David saw him. The prophet Gad told him to raise up an altar there. That day David purchased the property saying, *"I will not offer unto God that which costs me nothing."* It was on this spot Solomon built the Temple of the Lord. Today it is in the hands of the Moslems; but soon Jesus, the son of David, will rule and reign from there. Read the story in 2 Samuel 24 and 1 Chronicles 21-22. So we see that God can make something good and wonderful out of our wrongs. There would be no Israel today if it had not been for the terrible price of the Holocaust.

One of the things people have the most difficulty forgiving themselves for is that they have had an abortion. God has entrusted them with the gift of a new life from Heaven, the greatest gift God can give. But in fear, or because of shame, or the desire for freedom, there is no room in the heart for this gift— so there is no room in the womb, and the woman feels she must get rid of "it." She goes to those who promise to help her, but it is not a house of life, hope and help; it is a "slaughter house." They don't give her time to think about the consequences, the guilt, and the pain she will suffer the rest of her life. Before she knows it, they have made her a murderer of her own child, and she has opened herself to the demon Molech.[1] the world has been filled with the blood of

1   MOʹLECH (*king*). The fire-god Molech was the tutelary deity of the children of Ammon, and essentially identical with the Moabitish Chemosh. Fire-gods appear to have been common to all the Canaanite, Syrian, and Arab tribes, who worshipped the destructive element under an outward symbol, with the most inhuman rites. According to Jewish tradition, the image of Molech was of brass, hollow within, and was situated without Jerusalem. 'His face was (that) of a calf, and his hands stretched forth like a man who opens his hands to receive (something) of his neighbor. And they kindled it with fire, and the priests took the babe and put it into the hands of Molech, and the babe gave up the ghost.' Many instances of human sacrifices are found in ancient writers, which may be compared with the description in the Old Testament of the manner in which Molech was worshipped." Smith, W. (1997). *Smith's Bible dictionary*. Nashville: Thomas Nelson.

And they built the high places of Baal, which are in the valley of the son of Hinnom, to cause their sons and their daughters to pass through the fire unto Molech; which I commanded them not,

unborn children. Molech has turned the wombs of millions of mothers into death cells.

St. Paul, who had mercilessly persecuted the Christians, and even caused the death of some, wrote his spiritual son, Timothy, *"I thank Christ Jesus our Lord, who hath enabled me, for that he counted me faithful, putting me into the ministry; [13] Who was before a blasphemer, and a persecutor, and injurious: but I obtained mercy, because I did it ignorantly in unbelief. [14] And the grace of our Lord was exceeding abundant with faith and love which is in Christ Jesus [15] This is a faithful saying, and worthy of all acceptation, that Christ Jesus came into the world to save sinners; of whom I am chief"* (1 Timothy 1:12-15).

So if you have sinned or done something you know has grieved the Lord, fast, pray, and leave your burden at the feet of Jesus. Trust Him to turn it into good. Remember that even Jesus fell beneath the burden of carrying the cross, and this gave Simon, a Cyrenian, the honour of carrying it for Him because the Roman soldiers commanded him to do so (Matthew 27:32). Today Cyrene is called Libya, Africa. It was an African Jew who carried Jesus' cross. According to Mark 15:21, he was the father of Alexander and Rufus. Rufus is mentioned

neither came it into my mind, that they should do this abomination, to cause Judah to sin" (Jeremiah 32:35).

in Romans 16:13. He was living in Rome. Paul gives him a special greeting. Accept the cross of your mistakes, and it will lift you higher.

When you have repented and confessed your sin, forsake your old habits. You have learned your lesson. Go on from there. Don't look back. Jesus died for that sin also. *"He was numbered with the transgressors and he bare the sin of many, and made intercession for the transgressors"* (Isaiah 53:12b).

God has forgiven you! Now it is time for you to forgive yourself. Preacher, you may have been caught with your head on Delilah's lap; you may have been betrayed by the woman you loved, blinded, and forced to do donkey's work, grinding grain in the prison; take courage—your hair will grow again. Your future will be more glorious than your past.

When We Forgive, It Makes Our Lives Fruitful

Joseph suffered many years of abuse from his brothers. When his father, Jacob, sent him to his brothers, they wanted to kill him; it was only by the intervention of Reuben that his life was spared. They sold him to the Ishmaelites for twenty pieces of silver (Genesis 37:28). He was put on the slave block in Egypt, where he was purchased

by Potiphar, a good man with a lustful wife who
tried to seduce him. Wrongly accused, he was put
in prison for more than two years. When Pharaoh
heard of his gift of interpreting dreams, he sent for
him, and appointed him as governor over all Egypt.
He arranged a marriage for him, and God blessed
him with a son whom he named Manasseh, which
means "forgotten," *"For God, said he, hath made me
forget all my toil, and all my father's house"* (Genesis
41:51).

Then he had a second son whom he called
Ephraim: "doubly fruitful," *"For God hath caused
me to be fruitful in the land of my affliction"* (Genesis
41:51-52).

We can only get the double portion after we have
dealt with the sin of unforgiveness in our lives.
We have to believe that God had a purpose for it
all. Much later, when their father died, Joseph's
brothers were afraid he would punish them for all
the evil they had done to him. They sent an advocate
to plead their case, and they themselves came and
knelt down before him, begging his forgiveness. He
comforted them, *"Fear not: for am I in the place of
God? But as for you, ye thought evil against me; but
God meant it unto good, to bring to pass, as it is this
day, to save much people alive. Now therefore fear
ye not: I will nourish you, and your little ones. And*

he comforted them, and spake kindly unto them" (Genesis 50:19-21).

When you forgive, and forget, you will receive a baptism of love that will make your life fruitful in your "land of affliction."

Learn How to Forgive from a Child

The disciples of Jesus were discussing who among them would have the highest position in the New Kingdom which they expected Jesus would then set up in Jerusalem. Jesus interrupted their argument by setting a little child in their midst and saying, *"Verily I say unto you, Except ye be converted, and become as little children, ye shall not enter into the kingdom of heaven. Whosoever therefore shall humble himself as this little child, the same is greatest in the kingdom of heaven. And whoso shall receive one such little child in my name receiveth me"* (Matthew 18:1-5).

A young child is humble enough to forgive. He will never hold a grudge against anyone. He will put his arms around the one who has spanked him. He will just keep on loving and forgiving until his soul is crushed through continuous abuse and harshness. I believe the child can more easily forgive because it has not been a long time since he left Heaven, and the light and love of God is still remaining in him.

True greatness therefore comes from our willingness to be like a forgiving child. A child does not seek for honour or fame. He still has the fragrance of Heaven.

Why Is It So Hard to Say, "I Am Sorry?"

I believe that pride keeps many souls out of Heaven. We do not want to admit we could be wrong, or that we could be at fault. We have grown up putting the blame on someone else.

The Bible says, *"If we say that we have no sin, we deceive ourselves, and the truth is not in us. If we confess our sins, he is faithful and just to forgive us our sins, and to cleanse us from all unrighteousness. If we say that we have not sinned, we make him a liar, and his word is not in us"* (1 John 1:8-10).

Beloved, let us be honest with ourselves. Hamlet said in Shakespeare's well- known play, "This above all: to thine own self be true."

Don't let three little words (I AM SORRY) keep you from making peace with God, your neighbor, and your own heart. If you have sin in your heart, you will not have faith that God will answer your prayers. 1 John 3:21-22 says, *"Beloved, if our heart condemn us not, then have we confidence toward God. And whatsoever we ask, we receive of him, because we keep his commandments, and do those things that are pleasing in his sight."* Unconfessed sin will lock the door of Heaven to you. Isaiah 59:2 says, *"But your iniquities have separated between you and your God, and your sins have hid his face from you, that he will not hear."* We would have so many more answers to our prayers and miracles in our lives if we could forgive those who offend us. When you can be humble enough to say you are sorry (even if you are not to blame), it will show the greatness of God in you. Jesus took on Himself all of our sins. Shall we not do likewise, if we want to be like Him?

Never Take Another Person's Offences on Yourself

It is very easy to take on yourself somebody else's offences. When somebody who is dear to you is a victim of a bully, a slanderer, or a jealous person, and you see your friend suffer, you immediately feel you have to become involved in order to prove your loyalty. This can appear to be the right thing to do—but it is not always true. It can open your heart to many different kinds of negative emotions, such as anger, hatred, and gossip.

I remember hearing that a certain well-known minister spoke evil against a dear friend of mine.

I immediately took a strong dislike against that preacher. I held this feeling against him for quite a long time. Then one day I was visiting with my friend, and in our discussion, she mentioned her "friend" and added what wonderful fellowship they had when he visited her city. I was shocked. I never said a word, but I saw how wrong I had been to carry someone else's offences.

This does not mean that we should not defend someone who needs help. Peter denied that he knew Jesus three times before the rooster crowed, because he was a coward and afraid to be identified as one of His disciples. Peter suffered much because of what he did. He wept bitterly. And Jesus forgave him. In the case of Bob and Jenny, Jenny's brothers did the right thing. Many times family members know that a certain child is suffering sexual abuse from the father, or other members of the family, but they close their eyes to it, and refuse to intervene.

Never Seek for Companionship with a Busybody

The Bible warns us about busybodies who make it their life's task to spread gossip, and speak evil about others. They leave the place where they have ministered, travel to the next place, and immediately speak against the last church or minister. This is wrong. Never find yourself tearing down someone's character. And beware of the one who speaks evil against another—tomorrow they may do the same about you.

I remember traveling in the ministry through the country with someone who had that bad habit. I wasn't in a position to take authority against that person. We had left one place, where the people had been kind to us, and arrived at the next place. Before the evening meeting, we sat down to dinner with the pastor and his family. Immediately, my traveling companion began to speak negatively about the last place we had ministered. The pastor rebuked my companion, "We do not speak evil against others in this house!" It was spoken with firmness, and was like apples of gold (Proverbs 25:11). Proverbs 25:12 says, *"As an earring of gold, and an ornament of fine gold, so is a wise reprover upon an obedient ear."*

Paul exhorts his spiritual son Timothy, about young women who wander about *"from house to house; and are not only idle, but tattlers and busybodies speaking things which they ought not"* (1 Timothy 5:13).

To the Thessalonians, Paul writes, *"We hear that there are some which walk among you disorderly, working not at all, but are busybodies. [12] Now them that are such we command and exhort by our Lord*

Jesus Christ, that with quietness they work, and eat their own bread. [13] But ye, brethren, be not weary in well doing. [14] And if any man obey not our word by this epistle, note that man, and have no company with him, that he may be ashamed" (2 Thessalonians 3:11-14).

And Peter admonishes, *"Let none of you suffer as a murderer, or as a thief, or as an evildoer, or as a busybody in other men's matters... For the time is come that judgment must begin at the house of God: and if it first begin at us, what shall the end be of them that obey not the gospel of God?"* (1 Peter 4:15, 17).

There are so many good and wonderful things to talk about, why do we want to grovel in the garbage dump and throw mud balls about another child of God? We need to *"remember the rock from whence we are hewn, and the hole of the pit from which we have been digged"* (Isaiah 51:1).

St. Paul exhorts his beloved church at Philippi, *"Finally, brethren, whatsoever things are true, whatsoever things are honest, whatsoever things are just, whatsoever things are pure, whatsoever things are lovely, whatsoever things are of good report; if there be any virtue, and if there be any praise, think on these things."* (Philippians 4:8).

When Do We Dare to Speak Evil Against Another Person?

There are times when the saints need to be warned about certain troublemakers and avoid them.

Paul warned Timothy about two men whom he had delivered unto Satan because they had committed blasphemy, and made shipwreck of people's lives (1 Timothy 1:19-20). In his second letter to Timothy, he warned him about Alexander the coppersmith, who had done him much evil, and added, *"The Lord reward him according to his work"* (2 Timothy 4:14b).

In the book of Revelation, Jesus, speaking to the church, warns them about a woman He calls Jezebel, who calls herself a prophetess, who teaches the saints to commit fornication, and to eat things sacrificed unto idols (Revelation 2:20-23).

Over and over again, Jesus warns His disciples about the leaven (wrong teachings and the deeds) of the Scribes and Pharisees.

When Do We Keep Silent?

Love covers a multitude of sins. Women who refuse to reveal the sins or shortcomings of their husbands to the world are wise women. Always remember that your children still carry his name, even though you may be divorced and gone back to your maiden name or married another man. If you are still married to a fornicator you do not want to dirty the nest you are living in, and you don't want to put that "mark of Cain" on your children's lives. It will be like a chain around their necks.

I was showing a photo of a certain family to a woman of God in Germany. She took one look, and putting her finger on the man in the photo, said, "He is not a good man." I was amazed. I knew the man, and I knew that what she said was true. No matter how much "charm" we may use to impress others in a favourable way, we can never deceive the discerning eye of the anointed seer.

When do we keep silent? Most of the time. *"If any man among you seem to be religious, and bridleth not his tongue, but deceiveth his own heart, this man's religion is vain"* (James 1:26). James devotes the entire third chapter to the power of the tongue—*"for good and for evil."*

I remember talking with a brother who had worked for years with a well-known minister. When I asked him about that minister, he answered me, "I could say many things, but some day I will need mercy, and so I must take care what I say." That was a good rebuke to me, which I have never forgotten.

St. James warned us in James 2:13 *"For he shall have judgment without mercy, that hath shewed no mercy; and mercy rejoiceth against judgment."*

Words Can Cause Great Harm or Bring Beautiful Healing

When I was a child, we were taught "Sticks and stones can break my bones, but angry words can't hurt me." But that is not the entire truth. Unkind words can cause deep wounds to the soul. They can sow seeds of bitterness and anger that leave you reeling in pain, till you find yourself living in a cesspool of unforgiveness and hatred which you will pass on to others because you can't stop talking about your grievances. You will vent your anger on those whom you love, your spouse, your children, your parents, your neighbours, co-workers—just anyone. Its roots grow longer and stronger from generation to generation, bringing a curse that will impact families for generations. Words can split families and cause wars between nations.

I remember hearing about two sisters who never spoke to each other, even though they lived side by side, each in her own house. They built a high wall between their houses. I don't know if they ever made up.

Several years ago, I had a burden for the Mafia. After preaching one evening in Barcelona, the pastor put me and Linda, my interpreter, in a nice car and asked the driver to take us to the pastor's home. When the driver got into the car, the Holy Spirit told me that he had been a Mafioso. He spoke a little broken English. He said to me, "If you knew who I was you wouldn't get in my car." I smiled, because I already knew, but I played ignorant. And then he told me how his family had been in the Mafia for years. I felt his was a confirmation that I was to minister to these people. They were the very ones God had laid on my heart. He told me that his mother and father had lived in the same house, but had not spoken to each other for over thirty years. After my driver got saved in Spain, he went back to Sicily, and led his parents to the Lord. When they were born again, they ended their strife and became friends. Now they began walking down the street every evening, arm in arm. When the neighbours saw it, they were in shock. It impacted the whole town. One of Satan's strongholds was broken through forgiveness.

It Is Time for the Bride to Make Herself Ready for Her Wedding Day

It is time to forgive. If you want to be ready when the Bridegroom comes, you have to get rid of the poison of old, unforgiven offences. Remember when

John describes the wedding of Jesus and the Bride it says, *"Let us be glad and rejoice, and give honour to him: for the marriage of the Lamb is come, and his wife hath made herself ready"* (Revelation 19:7).

In order to be ready, the Bride of Christ must have forgiven everyone. It is time to be honest with yourself; do some true heart searching. Stop blaming others when people do not want to be with you. It could be that they feel the bitterness that is in you because of words you have spoken against someone they love. The root of bitterness is very hard to deal with because it is underground and grows in a dark place where it can suck up the water of bitterness that is poisonous enough to kill, like the Waters of Marah (bitterness) in the wilderness. The Children of Israel could not drink this poisonous water until the Lord showed Moses a tree, which Moses cut down and cast into the water to heal it. It was made sweet. This was a prophetic symbol that it is only through the Cross that healing can come to the bitter memories of your life. When He healed the waters through the tree, God made a covenant with them, *"If thou wilt diligently hearken to the voice of the Lord thy God, and wilt do that which is right in his sight, and wilt give ear to his commandments, and keep all his statutes, I will put none of these diseases upon thee, which I have brought upon the Egyptians: for I am the Lord that healeth thee"* (Exodus 15:26).

The Covenant Token of the Rainbow

God, at different times made different covenants with man. We wear a wedding ring as a token or sign of a covenant made between two parties. He made the Noahic Covenant with Noah, for which He gave the token of the rainbow (Genesis 9:12-17).

The Collins English Dictionary defines rainbow as, "a bow-shaped display in the sky of the colours of the spectrum, caused by the refraction and reflection of the sun's rays through rain or mist."[2] The light of God's love shining on our broken hearts turns our hurts and suffering into an opportunity for God to display His love to the whole world through our lives when we accept the pains, criticisms, misunderstandings, rejection, and abuse into an opportunity to suffer with Christ; otherwise, how can we be glorified with Him?

After the flood, Noah made a sacrificial love offering to God which pleased Him so much that He promised Noah, in Genesis 9:12-17: *"And God said, This is the token of the covenant which I make between me and you and every living creature that is with you, for perpetual generations: [13] I do set my bow in the cloud, and it shall be for a token of a covenant between me and the earth. [14] And it shall come to pass, when I bring a cloud over the earth, that the bow shall be seen in the*

2   *The Collins English Dictionary,* 2nd Edition, s.v. "rainbow," (London & Glasgow, William Collins Sons & Co. Ltd., 1979, 1986), 1263.

cloud: [15] And I will remember my covenant, which is between me and you and every living creature of all flesh; and the waters shall no more become a flood to destroy all flesh. [16] And the bow shall be in the cloud; and I will look upon it, that I may remember the everlasting covenant between God and every living creature of all flesh that is upon the earth. [17] And God said unto Noah, This is the token of the covenant, which I have established between me and all flesh that is upon the earth."

The light of God's love beamed out of His big God-heart upon a broken, destroyed, ruined world that was ugly and devastated. The only beautiful thing was the rainbow in the sky, a token of better days to come.

Do you feel you have reached a dead-end street, and you can't go on any longer? Look at the rainbow, and take it as God's personal promise to you. God will never leave you nor forsake you (Hebrews 13:4, Matthew 28:20).

The Covenant Token of Circumcision God Made with Abraham

God made a Covenant with Abraham in which He promised that He would give his descendents the land of the Canaanites, much riches, and Sarah would bare him a son, but Abraham, all his male descendents, and the men of his household had to be circumcised. He also changed his name from Abram to Abraham and Sarai's to Sarah (Genesis 17:1-14). Why the difference? God changed the meanings of their names by adding the Hebrew letter HEI (ה), a mystical letter in the Hebrew alphabet which is very powerful because it is the symbol of Divinity. You can't say it without breath. It has the breath of life in it.

When God created Adam, he was a beautiful and marvelous work of creation, but it wasn't until God breathed into him the breath of life that he became a living soul. *"And the Lord God formed man of the dust of the ground, and breathed into his nostrils the breath of life; and man became a living soul"* (Genesis 2:7). So adding the letter that is pronounced by the exhalation of breath imparts life.

Abram means "a high father; the exalted father; high and lofty thinker; high or honored father."

Abraham means "Father of a multitude; father of mercy, a father of many nations."

Sarai means "contentious, quarrelsome, my ruler, my princess."

Sarah means "princess; chieftainess, noble woman, to lead, to fight, a ruler." It was used by women of nobility.

The Hebrew sages say "that God used the letters ׳ [*yod*] and ה [*hei*] which form the Divine Name יה, Y*AH*, to create the universe. With the letter ׳ [*yod*] He created the World to Come, while with the ה [*hei*] He created This World (*Menachos* 29b). The sound of ה [*hei*] is a mere exhalation of breath, *hei*; it requires little effort, no movement of lip, tongue, or mouth (*Tanachuma Bereishis* 16). This effortless enunciation symbolizes the effortless creation—as the Psalmist testifies:... '*By the word of H*ASHEM *the heavens were made, and the breath of His mouth all their hosts*' (Psalm 33:6)." [3]

By adding this letter to their names God changed their bodies, making them younger, breathing new life into them. Suddenly, youth returned to both of them. Abraham got back the testosterone he had lost to old age, and Sarah felt like a young bride. Her youthful beauty returned again. In fact, she was so young and beautiful that Abimelech, the king of Gerar took her into his harem intending to make her one of his wives, if God had not stopped him (Genesis 20:1-18).

Suddenly Abraham felt young again, a thing which Sarah laughed at when the Lord visited them at their tent (Genesis 18:12), and told them they

---

3   Rabbi Michael L. Munk, *The Wisdom in the Hebrew Alphabet* (Brooklyn, NY: Mesorah Publications, Ltd. 1983), 85.

would have a son within a year's time. She said, *"After I am waxed old shall I have pleasure, my lord* [Abraham] *being old also."* Sarah was ninety years old and Abraham was one hundred. They had their second honeymoon because the breath of life was breathed into them through the changing of their names. That is why it is very important what names we give to our children. Make sure they are names that have a good spiritual meaning. And it is even more important that we have the breath of God in our souls.

Sarah lived another thirty-seven years. After she died, Abraham married another woman, Keturah, who bore him six sons. He also had concubines who bore him children (Genesis 25:1-6). After Isaac's birth, he lived seventy-five years—years that were packed full of life, love and vigour. They can't make drugs to match that today.

When God gave Abram the token of the covenant of circumcision, He changed his name and promised the Land of Canaan to his descendants. Abram agreeing to the cutting away of the flesh, even at the cost of great physical pain, put him into the position of obedience where God could bless him with His breath of new life to bring forth the child of promise.

The Token of Battle Scars

When God wants to do something new in a person's life He not only may change their name, it may also be a time of spiritual warfare and struggle. When Jacob began his journey back home from Haran, the Angel of the Lord met him and wrestled with him all night. Jacob said, *"I will not let thee go except thou bless me."* He blessed him in Genesis 32:22-32 and changed his name from Jacob (he will supplant, one who trips up others) to Israel (prince with God, soldier of God, God will rule, ruling with God, one who prevails with God). By touching his thigh, the Angel of the Lord broke Jacob's physical strength, so that from then on he had to rely on God. That Jacob had amazing strength was evident from the fact that he rolled the stone from the mouth of the well that had taken many men to do (Genesis 29:1-10), but now he had to trust God to give him supernatural strength. God also had to break his pride and caused him to limp from then on. He had a face-to-face encounter with God. That's why he called the place Peniel, which means "I have seen God." You have to have a face-to-face encounter with God. You cannot hide from God and cover up anything that would displease Him or grieve the Holy Ghost.

When God changes a person's name it is because He also wants to change his character. During the night of wrestling, the Angel touched Jacob in the hollow of his thigh and dislocated his hip. So when Jacob's name was changed, his walk was also changed. When you are wrestling with God for your blessing, know that He has put it in your heart to press in and hang on so that He can change your character and make you one who can rule and reign with Him. You will never be the same.

The Covenant Token of the Law

The token of God's covenant with Israel through the mediation of Moses (Exodus 34:28) was the Tablets whereon the Ten Commandments were inscribed by the hand of God, Himself, on two tablets that were brought down from Heaven itself, not from the earth. According to ancient Jewish scribes, they were written on tablets of sapphire. As Moses was coming down the mountain, he saw that the people had given themselves to idolatry, worshipping a golden calf that Aaron had made, saying that this golden calf had brought them out of Egypt (Exodus 32). In anger (a problem Moses always had to deal with that got him into lots of trouble), Moses threw the tablets down and they fell down the mountain and smashed to bits. This was a terrible thing, because this was the marriage covenant (*ketubah*) between God and Israel, but it was broken because they had played whoredom with the idols of Egypt.

The calf was one of the idols of Egypt. At God's invitation Moses went back up the mountain where for 40 days and nights he fasted and interceded for Israel. God was going to judge Israel and destroy them, but in answer to Moses' travail (Exodus 33-34), God told him that this time he had to hew out and bring the tablets, so "works" was added to grace and ever since then, that's what the Old Covenant has been about: works, works, works. And God in His mercy wrote out of Heaven on man-made tablets a second set of the high and holy laws called the ten commandments. It was the second edition. They were kept in the Ark of the Covenant in the Holy of Holies.

The Holy Communion, the Covenant Token of the Followers of Jesus Christ

We, who are believers and followers of Jesus Christ, have also been given a covenant sign. It is not the cross, or a manner of dress, nor many other things which are good, but it is The Holy Communion. It takes us straight to the Throne of God.

At the last Passover Supper with His disciples in the Upper Room, Jesus taught them how to observe the Holy Communion. He gave the pattern which we still follow today.

Later, the Holy Spirit inspired Paul to write to the church in Corinth the importance of Holy Communion in 1 Corinthians 11:23-32, with strict warnings that it must be taken with deep reverence and a pure heart.

"For I have received of the Lord that which also I delivered unto you, That the Lord Jesus the same night in which he was betrayed took bread: [24] And when he had given thanks, he brake it, and said, Take, eat: this is my body, which is broken for you: this do in remembrance of me. [25] After the same manner also he took the cup, when he had supped, saying, This cup is the new testament [covenant] *in my blood: this do ye, as oft as ye drink it, in remembrance of me. [26] For as often as ye eat this bread, and drink this cup, ye do shew the Lord's death till he come.*

Then Paul gives a stern warning: [27] *"Wherefore whosoever shall eat this bread, and drink this cup of the Lord, unworthily* [irreverently], *shall be guilty of the body and blood of the Lord. [28] But let a man examine himself, and so let him eat of that bread, and drink of that cup. [29] For he that eateth and drinketh unworthily, eateth and drinketh damnation to himself, not discerning the Lord's body. [30] For this cause many are weak and sickly among you, and many sleep* [die]. *[31] For if we would judge ourselves, we should not be judged. [32] But when we are judged, we are chastened of the Lord, that we should not be condemned with the world"* (1 Corinthians 11:23-32).

Never Take the Holy Communion Unworthily

Taking the Holy Communion is a very high and solemn act and must be done in a reverential way, by first repenting for all wrongs we have committed, or sins we don't want to acknowledge we have committed. Sins of omission (not doing something we should do) are as wrong as sins of commission (doing something we shouldn't do).

Paul is warning us that if we take the Holy Communion without first of all dealing with the sins and wrongs in our lives, we are offending God by coming to Him without first making restitution with Him and others. It is the same as if we are crucifying Jesus all over again. And for this there will be great judgment. We must judge our own selves before we approach a Holy God. Because many had turned the Lord's Holy Communion into a kind of "church party," not realizing how holy an ordinance it was, they were punished. Either they judged themselves or God judged them with sickness and death. Apparently, some believers had already died because of their disrespect for the Holy Communion.

The Message Bible explains it this way in 1 Corinthians 11:17-22: *[17-19]Regarding this next item, I'm not at all pleased. I am getting the picture that when you meet together it brings out your worst side instead of your best! First, I get this report on your divisiveness, competing with and criticizing each other. I'm reluctant to believe it, but there it is. The best that can be said for it is that the testing process will bring truth into the open and confirm it. [20-22]And then I find that you bring your divisions to worship—you come together, and instead of eating the Lord's Supper, you bring in a lot of food from the outside and make pigs of yourselves. Some are left out, and go home hungry. Others have to be carried out, too drunk to walk. I can't believe it! Don't you have your own homes to eat and drink in? Why would you stoop to desecrating God's church? Why would you actually shame God's poor? I never would have believed you would stoop to this. And I'm not going to stand by and say nothing.*

We need to realize that when we take Holy Communion we are coming to the Judgment Seat of Christ. I remember how this truth impacted my life many years ago. I was preaching this message in a large church. The pastor's wife (let us call her Becky), and I spent many hours discussing and talking about a certain person who was a thorn in the flesh to all her co-workers in the ministry. I wasn't involved with that other woman, but listening to Becky's story I picked up her grievances. Now I had to preach this message on Communion Sunday. I warned everyone who had unforgiveness towards someone that they must make peace before they took the Holy Communion. But as the plate was brought to her, she took the Holy bread and drank the cup. It was the last time she could. Two weeks later, she was taken to the hospital in a coma. A short while later she passed away. I felt terrible.

To make it worse, the Lord said to me, "You are next."

I cried out to Him, "Lord, my children are little, and need me; what can I do?" He told me I had to ask forgiveness of certain people. I wrote letters, often to people who didn't even know me, but whom I had judged, and talked against. One letter I carried about in my purse for a week before I had the courage to mail it. But one by one, I cleaned the slate, and received the peace of God. That was a long time ago.

Sometimes the hardness of our hearts can bring sickness and death to innocent family members. The Lord led me to give this message of warning in a large church in Indonesia. I did not know that the former choir director had a serious controversy with the choir. He walked out in anger, and even stopped attending the church regularly. But that Sunday morning he had come to hear me preach. He also partook of the Holy Communion without first making peace. The next day he came to me in the early morning prayer meeting, and asked me to pray for his one and only four- or five-year-old son who suddenly was very sick. They had taken him to the hospital. I did not know the details of his life, but when I laid my hands on him to pray for his little boy, the Holy Spirit told me that it was no use praying, God was going to take the child. We went to the hospital to see him. Doctors could do nothing for him. God took him. All his father's tears could not bring him back. At the grave of his son, weeping bitterly, he confessed that it was his hardness of heart and root of bitterness and anger that had killed his own child.

In my lifetime I have seen several tragic experiences that people have suffered which has caused untimely deaths, crippling diseases, etc. This does not mean that everyone who is sick or has died has unconfessed sin. Sometimes we are experiencing a "Job's trial." Always remember, the Holy Communion is either the place of forgiveness or the place of judgment—it all depends on how we participate. It can be our finest hour, a time of refining to make us pure and bring us into the Glory.

The Power to Forgive Is in the Blood of Jesus

There is a great mystery about blood. God gives great importance to it. The Lord spoke to Moses, and said, *"The life of the flesh is in the blood: and I have given it to you upon the altar to make an atonement for your souls: for it is the blood that maketh an atonement for the soul. [12] Therefore I said unto the children of Israel, No soul of you shall eat blood, neither shall any stranger that sojourneth among you eat blood"* (Leviticus 17:11-12).

God continued to instruct Moses, *"And whatsoever man there be of the children of Israel, or of the strangers that sojourn among you, which hunteth and catcheth any beast or fowl that may be eaten; he shall even pour out the blood thereof, and cover it with dust. [14] For it is the life of all flesh; the blood of it is for the life thereof: therefore I said unto the children of Israel, Ye shall eat the blood of no manner of flesh: for the life of all flesh is the blood thereof: whosoever eateth it shall be cut off"* (Leviticus 1:13-14). God even honours the blood of animals.

Cain, the first-born man on earth, was jealous of his brother. It was a religious jealousy, because God had accepted Abel's sacrificial offering, while He had rejected Cain's. When they were alone in the field, Cain slew his brother. The Lord said, *"'What hast thou done?' The voice of thy brother's blood crieth unto me from the ground"* (Genesis 4:11). Shed blood still speaks; it speaks either a blessing, or a curse.

The blood of Abel cried out, "You are guilty of killing me." Think of the many aborted babies, and their blood crying out to God against all who are involved in their horrific deaths! It is frightening to think about it, and the consequences. Behind it all, there is an unseen greed for "blood money."

The writer of Hebrews says that we have *"come to Jesus the mediator of the New Covenant, and to the blood of sprinkling, that speaketh better things than that of Abel"* (Hebrews 12:24). The Blood of Jesus cries out, *"Father, forgive them; for they know not what they do"*! (Luke 23:34).

Blood still speaks today! St. John said in 1 John 5:8 *"There are three that bear witness in earth, the spirit, and the water, and the blood: and these three agree in one.*

Blood was so honoured that the eating of it was forbidden under the New Covenant (Acts 15:29).

Jesus' Blood is God's "Liquid Love," filled with His perfect, sinless, immortal life. Its power is Eternal because God is Eternal. It will never lose its power. It has the power to forgive all our sins, and to make us into a new creation.

The Breastplate of Judgment

God told Moses to make a breastplate of judgment whereon were the gemstones of the tribes of Israel (Exodus 28:15-30). *"Aaron shall bear the names of the children of Israel in the breastplate of judgment upon his heart, when he goeth in unto the holy place, for a memorial before the Lord continually"* (Exodus 28:29).

Never forget that it is only by the grace and mercy of God that we dare approach the Throne of God in prayer, for He is a High and Holy God, and we cannot come to Him in our own righteousness. *"For by grace are ye saved through faith; and that not of yourselves: it is the gift of God: [9] Not of works, lest any man should boast"* (Ephesians 2:8-9).

The High Priest was a type of Jesus, the true High Priest, Who took upon Himself all the sins of the world, past, present, and to come, when He hung on the cross. That is when His Father could not bear to look upon Him, for sin cannot come into His Presence. Jesus suddenly felt their intimacy cut off. He felt like the sinner feels who says in his heart there is no God—the person who is God-forsaken. Jesus cried out, *"My God, my God, why hast thou forsaken me?"* (Matthew

27:46). He is our Intercessor Who continually pleads for us before the Father. He is the Advocate Who cannot lose a case. It always gives me hope to know that Jesus is interceding for me before the Father. *"Wherefore he is able also to save them to the uttermost that come unto God by him, seeing he ever liveth to make intercession for them"* (Hebrews 7:25).

Your Trials Will Make You Bitter or Better

Your trials and testings will make you bitter or better. It is up to you. If you determine that God is allowing you to go through something you don't understand right now, know this: that God knows all about it.

I remember Corrie ten Boom, giving her testimony to a gathering of missionary women in Hong Kong, of her time in different Nazi Concentration Camps, including Ravensbrück, which was a death camp. It was amazing how she could speak without bitterness, because the greatness of God was in her. She quoted from the poem, "The Weaver" by Benjamin Malachi Franklin (1882-1965):

Not till the loom is silent,
And the shuttles cease to fly,
Shall God unfold the canvas,
And explain the reason why
The dark threads are as needful

In the Weaver's skillful hand
As the threads of gold and silver
In the pattern He has planned.

When you are going through a great trial, sometimes the only prayer you can pray is "Why, Lord, Why?" But as Basilia Schlink said so truthfully, "What reason cannot understand, faith accepts."

It is a good thing to start counting your blessings. It will surprise you what God has done for you. We all need to show more gratitude to God for the many wonderful things He has done for us. The grateful heart receives more blessings from God than the complaining, grumbling heart. It was because the Children of Israel complained in the wilderness that they had to stay there forty years until that generation died out.

How to Deal with Betrayal

The Collins English Dictionary defines "betray" as:

1. to aid an enemy of (one's nation, friend, etc.)... 2. to hand over or expose (one's nation, friend, etc.) treacherously to an enemy. 3. to disclose (a secret, confidence, etc.) treacherously. 4. to break (a promise) or be disloyal to (a person's

trust)... 8. To betray oneself, to reveal one's true character, intentions, etc....[4]

The betrayal of a friend is one of the most painful things one can experience. Yet most of us have experienced it in our lives. King David complained to the Lord about a certain close friend who had betrayed him in Psalm 55:12-14, *"For it was not an enemy that reproached me; then I could have borne it: neither was it he that hated me that did magnify himself against me; then I would have hid myself from him: [13] But it was thou, a man mine equal, my guide, and mine acquaintance. [14] We took sweet counsel together, and walked unto the house of God in company."*

I have experienced this painful sword in my life more than once. Most of the time I have not talked about it with anyone. But I feel I should, for the first time in my life reveal one of these experiences in my life, though I will change names of people and place.

I had a close friend of many years. We spent nights and afternoons in prayer with a group of us who were hungry for more of God and praying for revival. I trusted Roberta. We laughed together, cried together, and worked together on the mission field. After a while, I went on to other nations. One

4   *Collins,* s.v. "betray" 146.

of the countries in which I had preached extensively and experienced great moves of God was Indonesia. I had many friends there, and a great open door. So, when, after many years, I decided to return, I was confident that the doors would be open to me—as they had been before. But this time I found that no one wanted me in their churches. All made different excuses. The pastor who had opened the doors for me before had died. I could not understand what had happened. I spent some time fasting and praying in the city where my plane landed. The people I was living with had a piano. I sat down at the piano, and began to worship the Lord. I have always found comfort in music. That is when God gave me the theme chorus of my life:

> Let the love of my God shine through me;
> Let the beauty of Jesus men see;
> Let the pattern of the Son
> Be the one, the only one
> That men will see in me.

I knew I had to hide myself in the Love of God.

Later, I found out what had happened. My old "friend" had made a journey to that nation to preach. Everywhere she went, she spoke evil against me— spreading lies, rumours, and evil words. She was very successful in turning the hearts of the people against me. This not only shocked me, it was like a knife in my heart.

Paul wrote the church at Philippi in Philippians 1:15-18, *"Some indeed preach Christ even of envy and strife; and some also of good will: [16] The one preach Christ of contention, not sincerely, supposing to add affliction to my bonds: [17] But the other of love, knowing that I am set for the defense of the gospel. [18] What then? notwithstanding, every way, whether in pretence, or in truth, Christ is preached; and I therein do rejoice, yea, and will rejoice."*

I like the way *The Message* Bible interprets it, *"It's true that some here preach Christ because with me out of the way, they think they'll step right into the spotlight... They see me as their competition, and so the worse it goes for me, the better—they think— for them. So how am I to respond? I've decided that I really don't care about their motives, whether mixed, bad, or indifferent. Every time one of them opens his mouth, Christ is proclaimed, so I just cheer them on! And I'm going to keep that celebration going because I know how it's going to turn out...."* (Philippians 1:15-21).

It seems strange that someone would "fast out of strife," but that is what enemies of Paul did. Acts 23:12-13 records, *"And when it was day, certain of the Jews banded together, and bound themselves under a curse, saying that they would neither eat nor drink till they had killed Paul. [13] And they were more than forty which had made this conspiracy.'* Thank God, it was averted!

In Philippians 3:18-21 Paul once more speaks about his enemies, *"(For many walk, of whom I have told you often, and now tell you even weeping, that they are the enemies of the cross of Christ: [19] Whose end is destruction, whose God is their belly, and whose glory is in their shame, who mind earthly things.) [20] For our conversation is in heaven; from whence also we look for the Saviour, the Lord Jesus Christ: [21] Who shall change our vile body, that it may be fashioned like unto his glorious body, according to the working whereby he is able even to subdue all things unto himself."*

How can you be glorified if you destroy that brother or sister for whom Christ died through your tongue? I really believe Roberta was jealous of the great things God was doing in my life. She literally was "preaching Christ out of envy."

Suicide: Another Form of Betrayal

One of the most condemning and hard to forgive situations is when a family member or a loved one commits suicide. It leaves an indelible mark on your soul and an open door for the adversary to condemn you the rest of your life that you have somehow failed that person, even though you may not have any way caused such a horrible thing to happen. People who go through these things often have to go for psychiatric care. But this is beyond the aid of man, because you are dealing with demons. You can often trace a history of suicide through past generations of the person who is a victim. This is caused by what is called a familiar spirit or a family demon that follows a family line. And so you need more than just counselling and prayer.

The demons that tried to destroy that boy in Matthew 7:14-21 by making him fall in the fire and in the water were suicide demons that were trying to end his life. Jesus' disciples weren't able to cast it out. Jesus upbraided them for their unbelief, but also explained that *"this kind goeth not out but by prayer and fasting"* (verse 21).

A very dear friend of mine lost two of her children through suicide. First her son committed suicide by shooting himself, then not too long after that, her twenty-year-old daughter took her life by asphyxiating herself in her mother's car shut up in the garage (an even more personal offence). And yet my friend seemed to live in joy. I asked her how she did it. She said, "I went to the grave and forgave my daughter and God gave me his peace." Many years later she discovered that her own father had died by suicide. It was a family secret that had been kept from her. If there has been suicide in your family in the past, guard yourself from that demon. Don't allow self-pity in your heart and pray and watch over your children.

Suicide is cruel because it really is an act of betrayal towards the ones that are left behind to deal with it. It also is an act of accusation. Many children have felt that their father or their mother did not love them or they wouldn't have left them.

Healing for You When You Are Betrayed

What did Jesus do on the night He was betrayed? Paul received this revelation from the Lord Jesus Himself. Paul says in 1 Corinthians 11:23-25 *"For I have received of the Lord that which also I delivered unto you, That the Lord Jesus the same night in which he was betrayed took bread: And when he had given thanks, he brake it, and said, Take, eat: this is my body, which is broken for you: this do in remembrance of me. After the same manner also he took the cup, when he had supped, saying, This cup is the new testament in my blood: this do ye, as oft as ye drink it, in remembrance of me."*

Taking Holy Communion will heal the broken heart. It will give you moral and physical strength, and the courage to walk into your future, no matter how dark it may seem to be. It will give you the courage to cross the swelling tide of the Jordan called Death. That is why the Church has ministered the Last Rites on the deathbed. The bread has been made into wafers so light and thin they can melt in the mouth. The wine or grape juice can be ministered with an eye-dropper; just one drop is enough, so there is no danger of choking. It is called "the anointing of the sick." More recently they realized it is wrong to wait until the person is dying to pray this anointing prayer. They believe if God can heal through the Holy Communion (and there are testimonies that He has), why wait? So the sick person comes to the altar, and the priest serves them the Eucharist and prays for their healing, believing that Christ has entered into them, bringing them healing through His wounded body, and forgiveness for their sins through the shed Blood of Christ.

The Roman Catholic Church and some of the High Episcopalian churches believe in the literal "transubstantiation" of the elements into the actual body and blood of Christ after the priest prays, "Make holy, therefore, these gifts, we pray, by sending down Your Spirit upon them like the dewfall, so that they may become for us the Body and blood of our Lord, Jesus Christ." Then they continue by quoting the story of the Holy Communion from the Scripture.

I'd like to quote this portion of Scripture, which Paul received from the Lord from *The Message* Bible: " *23-26Let me go over with you again exactly what goes on in the Lord's Supper and why it is so centrally important. I received my instructions from the Master himself and passed them on to you. The Master, Jesus, on the night of his betrayal, took bread. Having given thanks, he broke it and said,*

"This is my body, broken for you.
Do this to remember me.
After supper, he did the same thing with the cup:
This cup is my blood, my new covenant with you.
Each time you drink this cup, remember me.

"What you must solemnly realize is that every time you eat this bread and every time you drink this cup, you reenact in your words and actions the death of the Master. You will be drawn back to this meal again and again until the Master returns. You must never let familiarity breed contempt" (1 Corinthians 11:23-26).

Unforgiveness Can Keep You Out of Heaven

Most of us can say The Lord's Prayer by memory, but few remember the admonition Jesus spoke immediately after teaching us how to pray. He added very important words of warning, *"For if ye forgive men their trespasses, your heavenly Father will also forgive you: [15] But if ye forgive not men their trespasses, neither will your Father forgive your trespasses"* (Matthew 6:14-15).

Those are very serious words; and we all need to admonish our own hearts by true, honest soul-searching. Don't say to yourself, "When I get to Heaven I will be perfect." Now is the time to prepare your heart for eternity.

Ecclesiastes 11:3b says, *"If the tree fall toward the south, or toward the north, in the place where the tree falleth, there it shall be."* Dying will not make you holy. As you lived—so you shall die. If you lived a life of sin, you will die in your sin.

I have attended funerals of hardened sinners who have lived sinful lives, been cruel and abusive; but when someone gives the eulogy, you would think a great saint had gone to Heaven!

Dying doesn't sanctify you. As you lived—so shall you die! But, thanks be to God, there is such a merciful thing as a death-bed conversion, if we are conscious.

The Last Act of Revenge of the Spirit of a Dying Man

Sometimes the soul makes a journey on earth when a person is dying, or has already been pronounced dead. My father had a strange experience one night when I was a little girl. He was awakened from a deep sleep by a hard slap on his backside. He sat up in bed and asked Mother, "Bessie, why did you hit me?" He woke her up.

She answered him, "Ed, I never touched you." He said that someone had struck him an angry blow. The next day we got the news that a man, on whose farm we had lived for a short while, had died in the night. Apparently, that man and my father had had some disagreement, and the man had died with anger against my father. I never forgot that. You never know when the grim reaper will come for you, that is why it is important that you never go to bed angry. *"Let not the sun go down upon your wrath: [27] Neither give place to the devil"* (Ephesians 4:26b-27).

In my lifetime, I have heard of many such deathbed happenings. Get the garbage out of your life now before it is too late. I heard Corrie ten Boom say, "Corrie makes many mistakes, and is not perfect; but she knows what to do with her garbage;

she takes it to the Lord Who took upon Himself the sins of the world."

I lived in Hong Kong for seventeen years. I remember seeing metal containers that were attached to posts on which was the sign "RATS." People were expected to bring the rats they had managed to catch in a trap, or kill, and throw their dead bodies into the container. The sanitation department got rid of them. God has a place called The Cross, where we can bring our "rats." If we hang on to our past hurts and offences we can cause a plague to break out in our lives, our ministry, and our families that can last for many generations.

Enemy Number One

The worst enemy we have is one that goes with us wherever we go. St. James talks about this enemy in his powerful epistle. *"Even so the tongue is a little member, and boasteth great things. Behold, how great a matter a little fire kindleth! [6] And the tongue is a fire, a world of iniquity: so is the tongue among our members, that it defileth the whole body, and setteth on fire the course of nature; and it is set on fire of hell. [7] For every kind of beasts, and of birds, and of serpents, and of things in the sea, is tamed, and hath been tamed of mankind: [8] But the tongue can no man tame; it is an unruly evil, full of deadly poison. [9] Therewith bless we God, even the Father; and therewith curse we men, which are made after the similitude of God. [10] Out of the same mouth proceedeth blessing and cursing. My brethren, these things ought not so to be"* (James 3:5-10).

I would like to give it as it is recorded in *The Message*, beginning at verse three: *"A bit in the mouth of a horse controls the whole horse. A small rudder on a huge ship in the hands of a skilled captain sets a course in the face of the strongest winds. A word out of your mouth may seem of no account, but it can accomplish nearly anything—or destroy it!* 5-6*It only takes a spark, remember, to set off a forest fire. A careless or wrongly placed word out of your mouth can do that. By our speech we can ruin the world, turn harmony to chaos, throw mud on a reputation, send the whole world up in smoke and go up in smoke with it, smoke right from the pit of hell.*

*"*7-10*This is scary: You can tame a tiger, but you can't tame a tongue—it's never been done. The tongue runs wild, a wanton killer. With our tongues we bless God our Father; with the same tongues we curse the very men and women he made in his image. Curses and blessings out of the same mouth!* 10-12*My friends, this can't go on. A spring doesn't gush fresh water one*

day and brackish the next, does it? Apple trees don't bear strawberries, do they? Raspberry bushes don't bear apples, do they? You're not going to dip into a polluted mud hole and get a cup of clear, cool water, are you?" (James 3:3-12).

We are the master of the words we have not spoken, and the slave of the words we have. How important it is that we guard the words of our mouth. Jesus said in Matthew 5:37 *"Let your communication be, Yea, yea; Nay, nay: for whatsoever is more than these cometh of evil."*

My Father's Home-Going

When my father was dying of cancer in 1972, I came home from working behind the Iron Curtain because God told me He was going to take my father home, and He wanted him to bless me. We kept him at home. There was nothing that man could do for him anymore. As I saw the end approaching, I called his personal doctor and asked him if he could come to the house and give him oxygen.

He told me that it was his free weekend, and he would not come. He told me that I should call for an ambulance to take him to the hospital, and that if we didn't do it, he would begin to suffer great pain (up until then, he had not had any pain), and be in agony for at least two weeks—and I would be to blame for refusing to send him to the hospital. So I hung up the receiver, disappointed and sad, but still believing God was greater than that doctor's words of doom and gloom.

I picked up the old hymn book, walked into dad's bedroom, and started singing the beautiful old hymns about Heaven. Mother came in and joined me. Then Jim, who had flown in from California to help my mother take care of Dad and lift him, came and joined us. As we were singing, I was watching Dad. I saw him take his last breath, but I said nothing. My mother tried to communicate with him, so I had to tell her, "Dad has gone." I saw as his spirit stopped for a moment when he reached the ceiling, and looked back at us, and I said, "Thank you, Daddy, for praying for me when everybody said I was lost forever, and going to Hell." (I still remember how he told that church elder, "I will never stop praying for my daughter.")

I went back to the phone and called the doctor to tell him that my father had expired. He was shocked. He said, "In that case I will have to come." As I was waiting for him, I asked the Father, "How was it that my father did not suffer?" The Lord answered me, "When your father lived he never spoke an unkind word about anyone. He never repeated gossip—true or false that would injure anyone's character, nor cause pain. So I spared him pain and suffering."

When the doctor came, he checked out Dad and called the funeral home to send a hearse. He sat there, puzzled. I said to him, "A couple of hours ago, you told me how my dad will suffer more and more, until he dies in great pain. But I will tell you why he didn't suffer." And then I told him what the Lord had told me.

I pray that I may have the grace of God in my life to have this same gift of kindness and love in my mouth, *"for out of the abundance of the heart the mouth speaketh. [35] A good man out of the good treasure of the heart bringeth forth good things: and an evil man out of the evil treasure bringeth forth evil things. [36] But I say unto you, That every idle word that men shall speak, they shall give account thereof in the day of judgment. [37] For by thy words thou shalt be justified, and by thy words thou shalt be condemned"* (Matthew 12:34b-37).

We Need Enlargement of Heart

In Luke 14:15-24 Jesus told a parable about a certain man who made a great supper. When it was time to eat, he sent out his servants to escort the people who had been invited to the feast. But they refused to come. They had all kinds of excuses. The master of the feast was angry when he saw how they had rejected this wonderful, honourable invitation. He commanded his servants to go out to the lanes and streets of the city and bring in the poor, the maimed, the halt, and the blind. So they did that, and reported *"Yet there is room."*

The master of the house said, *"Go out into the highways and hedges. And compel them to come in, that my house may be filled. For I say unto you, That none of those men which were bidden shall taste of my supper."* How sad! Just to think that they would never be able to even "taste" the blessings of the wedding feast of the Lamb and His Bride.

If we lose our appetites for spiritual things, we won't know what we are missing. Two of my grandsons were visiting me for a picnic. I invited them to taste my pickles. One absolutely refused. But, I pursued with the other boy. After much talking and bribery, he tried a little piece. At first, he made a face. But when I offered him a second pickle, he accepted it without reluctance. He ended up enjoying grandma's pickles! So many have lost their appetite for spiritual things, and don't even realize it. I have seen teenaged boys look with scorn, at their mother's delicious home roasted turkey, and have gone out to eat hamburgers. This is the "hamburger generation."

Jesus Loved and Received Sinners:

1. The Samaritan woman at the well who had been married to five men, and was now living with a man who wasn't her husband (John 4).

2. The woman who came to Jesus when he was a guest at the house of a Pharisee, and brought an alabaster box of ointment, weeping, and washing His feet with her tears, and wiping them with the hairs of her head. He told her, *"Thy sins are forgiven"* (Luke 7:36-40).

3. The woman caught in the act of adultery. It was the Pharisees who brought her to Jesus, accusing her and quoting from the Old Covenant which demanded the punishment of death by stoning. Jesus took a while to answer their question as to what He recommended. He knew they were tempting Him, trying to get Him in trouble with the Law of the Romans who occupied the land. *"But Jesus stooped down, and with his finger wrote on the ground, as though he heard them not. [7] So when they continued asking him, he lifted up himself, and said unto them, He that is without sin among you, let him first cast a stone at her. [8] And again he stooped down, and wrote on the ground. [9] And they which heard it, being convicted by their own conscience, went out one by one, beginning at the*

eldest, even unto the last: and Jesus was left alone, and the woman standing in the midst. [10] When Jesus had lifted up himself, and saw none but the woman, he said unto her, Woman, where are those thine accusers? hath no man condemned thee? [11] She said, No man, Lord. And Jesus said unto her, Neither do I condemn thee: go, and sin no more" (John 8:1-11).

Besides the stories of these women, there were different men who Jesus forgave and healed at the same time.

We have to open our hearts to love the sinner, the prostitute, the drug addict, the prisoner, the sick and dying, the orphans, the beggars, the illegal immigrants, the foreigners, the gypsies, our enemies and their children, the alcoholic, sexual pervert, the sodomite, the transsexuals, the illegitimate child, the obnoxious person, the feeble-minded and physical and mentally handicapped, the one who gets on your nerves, the preacher who has fallen into sin—otherwise how can we help them? Jesus took upon Himself all their sins. He did not love their sins; He loved them. We hate the sin, but we love the soul who is a captive of Satan. Jude 1:21-23 exhorts us, *"Keep yourselves in the love of God, looking for the mercy of our Lord Jesus Christ unto eternal life. [22] And of some have compassion, making a difference: [23] And others save with fear, pulling them out of the fire; hating even the garment spotted by the flesh."*

Hebrews 9:28 tells us that Jesus offered Himself as a sacrifice to bear the sins of many. Many suffer nervous breakdowns because they are unloved. It is time to forgive and to love the cast-offs of society, many of whom are precious souls who are unwelcome in the church. It is time to love, even as God does (John 3:16). Never has the need to give love been so great.

Looking out the window one day, Rev. Dwight L. Moody and his friend saw an alcoholic tottering down the street. Moody's friend commented on how disgusting that man was. Moody responded, "There but for the grace of God, go I."

These are the lost souls in the streets, highways, and byways who will fill our Father's house. In the meanwhile, they are tomorrow's revivalists, missionaries, evangelists, Bible Teachers, and whatever God has planned for their lives.

Take an Honest Look at Yourself

We must be honest with ourselves. None of us is perfect. St. John, the Apostle of Love said, *"If we say that we have no sin, we deceive ourselves, and the truth is not in us. If we say that we have not sinned, we make him a liar, and his word is not in us"* (1 John 1:8, 10).

When things go badly, an accident happens, we or our children are sick, we look for someone to blame. We must stop justifying ourselves, and putting the blame on others. We have to recognize that we have an enemy who is always ready to split the camp, divide the families, and bring enmity between brothers.

A precious Christian couple who served the Lord couldn't get along. They were always arguing, until it was destroying their family. The husband told me how he had prayed and begged God to change his wife. Then one night he had a vision or dream in which he saw his wife and himself; in between them stood an ugly demon keeping them apart from each other. Then he knew who the trouble-maker was. It wasn't his wife, it wasn't himself; it was the accuser of the brethren. Paul says in Romans 16:17-18, *"Now I beseech you, brethren, mark them which cause divisions and offences contrary to the doctrine which ye have learned; and avoid them. [18] For they that are such serve not our Lord Jesus Christ, but their own belly; and by good words and fair speeches deceive the hearts of the simple."*

Guilty or Not Guilty, Take the Blame

Someone came to me and told me that a certain person had ought against me in their heart. My advisor counseled me how to answer. "Take the blame, just ask for forgiveness." So I did exactly that, though I could not understand. But as I looked back, I have to confess that my dedication to Christ has been so complete, that I have put Him first in my life to the hurt of other lives. My children, for example, suffered much because their mother was out preaching on some distant mission field, while their father and Chinese *amah* took care of them. So in a way, I am guilty of hurting even those whom I love the most.

Pride will hinder us from taking the blame. But when we reach the end of our lives we will understand—and so will those who accuse us without knowing the whole story of our pain and heartache. Sometimes the pain of being absent from my children was so great that I was ready to pack it up, go to the airport, and take the next flight home. Only dedication to God held me bound to my vows to God.

God Can Change a Heart in a Moment

After God gave me the double portion anointing, He began to use me in a new way. Lives were changed when I ministered. The Holy Spirit laid a burden on my heart to have revival meetings in a church where I had worked and ministered for several years. When I met the pastor on the street, I told him about my burden, and asked him if it would be possible for me to come and minister for a short while. We were good friends. But he had no faith. He told me that things were in such a state of division and enmity in the church that it wouldn't be a good thing to try to have a revival. He wanted to wait until they got their problems ironed out, and then he would call me. I felt sad. Didn't he know that the revival will take care of the problems, the fighting and disputes? That is what revival is all about. It brings to life that which has died. New love and unity flows in the heart. People get the mind of Christ. The Holy Spirit can do more to convict us of sin than hours of discussion.

When the Holy Spirit fell in Jerusalem, He cleaned up thousands of lives. One day Jesus came riding into the city on a donkey and the people hailed Him *"Blessed be the King that cometh in the name of the Lord: peace in heaven, and glory in the highest"* (Luke 19:38). One week later, the multitudes were screaming, *"Crucify Him! Crucify Him!"* Fifty days after that, when the Holy Spirit fell, three thousand repented, were baptized in water, and became the founders of the Early Church. You never know what

God can do with a hard, double-minded heart (Acts 2:22-23, 41).

The Greatness of God in David

At no time was the goodness and love that was in David's heart so clearly revealed than when he heard that his enemy, King Saul, who had tried to kill him many times, and made his life miserable for so many years, had died. He had forced David to live a life of wandering in the wilderness. Instead of shouting for joy, he wrote a requiem of love. It is found in 2 Samuel 1:19-27. I want to quote only verse 23, *"Saul and Jonathan were lovely and pleasant in their lives, and in their death they were not divided: they were swifter than eagles, they were stronger than lions."*

David was not perfect; he made many mistakes, yet, in one of his sermons Paul says that God called him *"a man after mine own heart, which shall fulfill all my will"* (Acts 13:22).

Things that Can Hinder You from Forgiving

Let us try to pin down the things that can hinder us from forgiving:

1. Being disillusioned. A friend whom we have trusted suddenly turning against us and working against us behind our backs can cause us to lose

faith in people. It can make us bitter, and angry. We must guard our hearts against this. Not all people are unfaithful.

2. Pride. We can easily become offended when someone says something against us to humiliate us. There are religions that kill their own daughters because they have offended their traditions, and call it "honour killing." The most recent accounts are 110 in Europe, eight or nine in Canada, and four in the USA.

3. Hardness of heart. Without love, it is very difficult to love enough to forgive someone who has wounded you. The wounds of the heart are much more difficult to forgive than physical wounds.

4. Saving face. It wasn't too many years ago, that the daughter was kicked out of the home if she got pregnant out of wedlock. She was left to roam on the streets. People called her all kinds of cruel names. The father of her unborn child would have nothing to do with her either. It will take a great grace of God for her to forgive.

5. A dishonest business partner can steal your money or misuse it, bringing you into bankruptcy. It is hard to forgive the one who has caused you to lose your home and all your life's hard earned possessions. The thief doesn't like to work. You work

hard to make ends meet, while your co-worker is secretly putting hundred dollar bills in his pocket. Many church ushers have even stolen from the church offerings.

There are many things that cause us to shut up our bowels of compassion, stopping the flow of God's love. When we do that, we cannot forgive, for without love we cannot forgive.

The Benefits of Forgiveness

There is a powerful chapter in the Bible about the blessing of love. It is Isaiah 58. The prophet Isaiah is rebuking the people for keeping laws and traditions, but lacking in love and charity. He is not calling us to religious tradition, but to the caring of the souls of men. This is what God is looking for us to have in our lives. *"Is not this the fast that I have chosen? to loose the bands of wickedness, to undo the heavy burdens, and to let the oppressed go free, and that ye break every yoke? [7] Is it not to deal thy bread to the hungry, and that thou bring the poor that are cast out to thy house? when thou seest the naked, that thou cover him; and that thou hide not thyself from thine own flesh?* God is not looking for a lot of rigid religious works and rules, but for loving hearts.

The reward for loving is very great. Read on!

Isaiah 58:8-12 should inspire us; *"Then shall thy light break forth as the morning, and thine health shall spring forth speedily: and thy righteousness shall go before thee; the glory of the Lord shall be thy rereward. [9] Then shalt thou call, and the Lord shall answer; thou shalt cry, and he shall say, Here I am. If thou take away from the midst of thee the yoke, the putting forth of the finger, and speaking vanity; [10] And if thou draw out thy soul to the hungry, and satisfy the afflicted soul; then shall thy light rise in obscurity, and thy darkness be as the noonday: [11] And the Lord shall guide thee continually, and satisfy thy soul in drought, and make fat thy bones: and thou shalt be like a watered garden, and like a spring of water, whose waters fail not. [12] And they that shall be of thee shall build the old waste places: thou shalt raise up the foundations of many generations; and thou shalt be called, The repairer of the breach, The restorer of paths to dwell in."*

Best of all, our natural and spiritual children will continue in laying the foundation for many generations to follow in the great things God has planned for their lives. And where people have gone astray, we will be enabled to bring unity where there has been a breach in a church or home or between two countries. We will be blessed to be used by God as His peacemakers; and be very close to Him. Jesus said, *"Blessed are the peacemakers: for they shall be called the children of God"* (Matthew 5:9) He also said, *"Blessed are the merciful: for they shall obtain mercy"* (Matthew 5:7).

Never be afraid to give to the needy. God is no man's debtor. You cannot outgive God. He has a bigger shovel than you have. You are laying up your treasures in Heaven.

The creative light of God will emanate from our lives, our health will improve speedily, the Glory of the Lord will be all around us. We will be wrapped up in the Glory of God, like Enoch was. When we pray, we will receive instant answers to prayers. The Lord will guide us so that we don't get out of His will for our lives. He will prosper our lives, and the water of life will flow out from us. We will not be empty cisterns, wells without water, or clouds without rain (Jeremiah 2:13, Jude 1:12).

Don't Be Offended by Those Who Leave You

To be forced to live through a split in the Church, a divorce, the loss of a friend or disciple, is very hard to understand. Jesus had many followers until He began to teach on the power of Holy Communion. *"From that time many of his disciples went back, and walked no more with him".* (John 6:66). This did not shock nor surprise Jesus. He knew the hearts of all men. He knew who would be faithful, and who would deny Him when they could not understand the deeper truths of Heaven (John 6:64).

Jesus knew that many had followed Him because they had eaten of the loaves and fishes. They were thrilled with the idea that they wouldn't have to work for a living anymore. They would follow Jesus, and He would feed them—even in the wilderness. The miracles had lost their attraction, now they had something better—prosperity! (John 6:26-27).

John was there that day when it happened, and he must have been thinking about it when he wrote in his epistle, *"They went out from us, but they were not of us; for if they had been of us, they would no doubt have continued with us: but they went out, that they might be made manifest that they were not all of us"* (1 John 2:19).

I believe that before we were born, our eternal spirits were in Heaven with our Father. He joined some of us together to fulfil a certain mission on earth, which we accepted. We do not remember, but then, neither do we remember our nine months in our mother's womb, yet, we were alive and heard everything our mother heard. If she loved a certain type of music, we were born with a preference for it. If she was a drug addict, we were born addicts. We have mortal, temporary senses for our physical bodies which are given to us for our life on earth; and we have spiritual senses which are eternal—even as our spirits are eternal. When we die, the body returns to dust, out of which it was made, the soul goes to the one who has been its master—God, or the devil, and the spirit is absorbed back into the Father of all spirits. *"Then shall the dust return to the earth as it was: and the spirit shall return unto God who gave it"* (Ecclesiastes 12:7). *"For the word of God is quick, and powerful, and sharper than any twoedged sword, piercing even to the dividing asunder of soul and spirit, and of the joints and marrow, and is a discerner of the thoughts and intents of the heart"* (Hebrews 4:12).

So, don't grieve too much when they break off from you. It could be that they never were in a covenant relationship with you when they joined up with you. Let them go! Send them off with a party. Let the "Hagars" of your life go with your gifts of bread and water. That's what Abraham did when he sent Hagar, his concubine, and their son, Ishmael, who was conceived of the flesh. He was not the son of promise, as Isaac was, of whom it was said, *"That in Isaac shall thy seed be called"* (Hebrews 11:18).

Never Reject the Repentant Sinner

When the prodigal son returned home, his one and only brother was angry and jealous because of the celebration. He felt his father ought to scold him and punish him—instead, he wept for joy. He was concerned about the waste of money. Instead of him having a burden for his brother's soul, he had a "burden" for the money. Let us get our priorities correct. The angels in Heaven rejoice over one sinner who repents, and the bells of Heaven start ringing—let us join in with them in the celebration (Luke 15:7, 10).

Don't Expect the New Christian to be Perfect

The first time I preached in Beaches Chapel in Jacksonville, Florida, I was thrilled to hear that God was working there in a spirit of revival. Jim and I were staying with Dr. Doug Fowler and his wife, Sue. Sue excitedly told me about how a backslidden trumpeter had come back to God. His father, who had been a Four Square Preacher, had passed away, but his mother, Ruth, was still living. They had prayed much for their son, Phil Driscoll. Phil was a professional Rock Musician for his generation. He had a recording studio, and a contract with a big music company to compose, teach, and record their artists. He also had a live-in girlfriend, Lynn. During the move of God, Phil had given his heart to the Lord. When I was preaching he came to one of the meetings.

One night, when the Spirit was high in the meeting, I suddenly was inspired to call for Phil to come to the platform and play the trumpet. He didn't have one with him, so he borrowed one from one of the musicians in the orchestra. As he began to play, *"How Great Thou Art,"* the Power of God fell on him, and he began to shake. Suddenly he broke out speaking in tongues, just like they did in the House of Cornelius, (Acts chapter ten). The Spirit of God fell on all in the chapel. After the meeting, he asked Jim and me to come and dedicate his Rock and Roll Recording Studio to God.

I wondered how I would do that! But the next day, when we got there, we found him sitting at the piano, composing worship music. God had changed his song. We went to prayer and took back from the devil all he had robbed for so long.

Then I found out that I was in trouble with some of the elders; for they had made the decision that they could not allow Phil to minister because he was "living in sin." So I had unknowingly broken this rule, when I invited him to come to the platform to play. I wasn't the only one in trouble—the Holy Ghost was too, because He had fallen in the middle of it all! But, God took care of that too, for Phil and Lynn were joined in a legal marriage, and after that, the platforms of the world were open to him. And, thank God, he was able to break his contract with the Music Company without much complication.

Don't expect your newly hatched birds to fly until they have developed strong wings.

Never Allow Unforgiveness to Destroy the High Calling of God on Your Life

Bitterness and unforgiveness can destroy your life and ministry. I am going to share something that changed my life.

Because of wrong choices I had made one year after my conversion, not from disobedience, but from ignorance, I suffered for many years. While working for the Lord on the mission field, and during furloughs I saw the weakness in the lives of Christian men which disgusted me. As a result, I lost respect for men—even Christian men. This disdain affected my preaching.

One Sunday morning, after preaching at a church in Tonawanda, New York, I returned home to my parents' house, where I was living while in America. I remember the scene, as though it happened yesterday. I was standing in the kitchen; my mother was basting the roast in the oven, when mom said words I will never forget. "That was a good message, but don't you think you were too hard on the men?"

"No, I don't! Except for Dad, I don't think there is one good man in the world," I answered.

"Oh yes, there are, and I am going to pray for you," answered my frank and outspoken mother. I pushed the subject into the background, thinking it was just the opinion of one person.

Several months later, while living in Chicago, a sister in Christ who was a dear friend came to me and said, "Sister Gwen, if you don't get your bitterness of men out of your heart, it will ruin your ministry."

This time I knew it wasn't just the opinion of my mother. God was trying to tell me something. But how do I change? God would have to help me.

Some time later, while ministering in Los Angeles, God visited me during my morning devotions. The Holy Spirit fell on me; I fell on my knees, weeping, when it happened. Suddenly, I was in The Garden of Eden, and I saw as the whole scene was re-enacted before me. I saw Eve being deceived by Satan, who had appeared to her as an angel of light, and I saw Eve enticing Adam into deception, and partaking of the forbidden fruit. I knew then, that men were like they were because the daughters of God had been used by the devil to destroy man who had been made in the image and likeness of God. Then God said to me, "I want you to love every man as though he were your brother." When He spoke those words I knew He was not only referring to my Christian brothers, but every man of every nation, tribe, and religion. God gave me a baptism of Love—Divine Love—that changed my life, and saved my ministry. Immediately after that, I began to preach about LOVE. For several years it was the only subject I preached on. It seemed that every verse in the Bible somehow led to LOVE.

It was also one week after that experience I met Jim Shaw while speaking at a Single Adults Breakfast Fellowship one Sunday morning in Santa Barbara. If it had not been for that baptism of love, I would never have been ready for the beautiful gift of love God had prepared for me in answer to my mother's prayers.

After our marriage, Jim and I lived in Germany, pastoring a small church and preaching in many places, besides smuggling Bibles behind the Iron Curtain. We were a team. The Heavenly Matchmaker had planned this life for us before we were born. After 33 wonderful years God took him

Home; but I feel His prayers for me, and I know he is waiting for me at the Eastern Gate.

I shudder to think what I would have missed if I had not been given the grace of God that took the bitterness and hurt out of my life, and helped me to forgive. I feel I got a new heart.

When we returned to America I wrote my greatest book, *Love, The Law of the Angels*. It is compiled from the sermons I preached in Germany and Switzerland during the year we lived there. (See page 115 and 128). None of my books have been more loved, and more criticized.

Why is it that when we lose our love for God, we make up rigid, religious Laws as a substitute? When we lose our first bridal love for Christ, we leave the New Covenant of love and liberty, and go back to the Old Covenant of laws and rules, trying to substitute something to ease our conscience and to please God. Instead of flying like a bird, we confine ourselves in a man-made cage, and give the religious demons the key to it.

Many are praying for a great revival to sweep the land. It can only begin when we have enough of the love of God in our hearts to be able to forgive. By forgiving we will fulfill all the Law. And we will find ourselves walking on the golden highway that leads straight back to the Heavenly Garden of Eden, from whence we came.

Come, take my hand, and walk with me this High Way of Forgiveness that leads to the Marriage Supper of the Lamb. Jesus is waiting for His Bride who has made herself ready by making all things right with her fellow pilgrims.

The Bridegroom is waiting. Come! *"And the Spirit and the bride say, Come. And let him that heareth say, Come. And let him that is athirst come. And whosoever will, let him take the water of life freely"* (Revelation 22:17).

COME! Begin your journey today by forgiving someone. And with a sincere heart, ask them to forgive you—even if you are not at fault. Take the blame. It will be worth it all. Your white, linen robe is waiting for you, dear Bride of Christ; but you can't wear it until you have bathed yourself in the baptism of love—holy, cleansing love that flowed in every drop of Jesus' blood.

The Spirit is calling; the Bride is calling to the few who yet remain to be brought in before the number is complete.

COME!

"And to Jesus the mediator of the new covenant, and to the blood of sprinkling, that speaketh better things than that of Abel" (Hebrews 12:24).

I love the song we used to sing in Canada:

An Evening Prayer
by C. Maude Battersby (written circa 1911)

If I have wounded any soul today,
If I have caused one foot to go astray,
If I have walked in my own willful way,
Dear Lord, forgive!

If I have uttered idle words or vain,
If I have turned aside from want or pain,
Lest I myself shall suffer through the strain,
Dear Lord, forgive!

If I have been perverse or hard, or cold,
If I have longed for shelter in Thy fold,
When Thou hast given me some fort to hold,
Dear Lord, forgive!

Forgive the sins I have confessed to Thee;
Forgive the secret sins I do not see;
O guide me, love me and my keeper be,
Dear Lord, Amen.

"Be ye therefore merciful,
as your Father also
is merciful…
forgive,
and ye shall be forgiven"

(Luke 6:36-37).

Life Changing Books from Engeltal Press

GWEN SHAW'S AUTOBIOGRAPHY!

UNCONDITIONAL SURRENDER—*Gwen Shaw.* The life story of Gwen R. Shaw, lovingly known as "Sister Gwen" to thousands of people in over one hundred nations. You will laugh and cry with her as you feel the heartbeat of a great woman of God who has given all to Him, asking only for souls in return. Your life will be challenged as you walk with her through mission field after mission field. You will never be the same when you read how God pours out His Spirit and confirms His Word ....**Paperback #000102 $14.00**

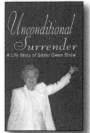

Video NTSC (North American format).............#GSLN-99 $20.00
Video PAL (European format).........................#GSLP-99 $20.00
DVD.. #GSLN-99D $20.00
Video PAL (European format) ....#GSLP-99 $20.00
Spanish Video NTSC .... #GSLN-99SP $20.00

> *Receive a word from God each day with a Devotional Book!*

DAILY PREPARATIONS FOR PERFECTION —*Gwen Shaw.* This daily devotional comes to you exactly as the Holy Spirit spoke to the author's heart in her own private devotions. You will feel that Jesus is speaking to you every time you open it. It is loved by all. You'll read it and re-read it! ....
....Paperback #000202 $12.50

DAY BY DAY—*Gwen Shaw.* This daily devotional book based on the Psalms will give you an inspiring word directly from the Throne Room each day to fill your heart with praise to God. Starting each day with praise is the secret of a joy-filled life............. Softcover #000204 $9.95
....Hardcover #000203 $18.50
French....................................Hardcover #000203FR $18.50
German...................................Softcover #000203GE $26.00

FROM THE HEART OF JESUS—*Gwen Shaw.* This devotional book is like no other. It will take you back to Bible days and you will walk and talk with Jesus and His disciples as he ministered to the people, as He suffered and died and as He rose again from the dead. These words from the heart of Jesus will go straight to your heart, bringing comfort, peace, encouragement and hope! 923 pages. Hardcover ....#000207 $29.95

GEMS OF WISDOM — A daily devotional based on the book of Proverbs — *Gwen Shaw.* In the Proverbs you will find instruction for upright living, honesty, justice and wisdom. Every word applies to today's problems as when they were first written. If you are facing problems which seem to have no solution, have a Proverb and an inspired writing about it for each day... Hardcover #000209 $25.95
French (2 Vol. Hardcover)........................#000209FR $54.00I

N THE BEGINNING — A daily devotional based on the book of Genesis — *Gwen Shaw.* The Book of Genesis is perhaps the most important Book in the Old Testament. It is the foundation stone of all knowledge and wisdom. Deep and wonderful truths hidden in the pages of Genesis are revealed in this devotional book. You'll be amazed at the soul-stirring writings inspired by the well-known stories of Genesis. Hardcover .... #000211 $27.95
French ....Hardcover #000211FR $27.95

HE SENT ME BACK TO TELL YOU — *Gwen Shaw.* While Sister Gwen's body was in intensive care, her spirit was standing at the gates of Heaven. The intercessors were asking God to send her back. He heard their cries and returned her to earth with a message. Before she left the hospital, she picked up her pen and notebook and began to record the words in this devotional book...#000213 $37.95

Other Books by Gwen Shaw

ASHTORETH—GODDESS OF LUST — *Gwen Shaw.* This temptress has worked for millennia through base carnal desires, fueling the fires of passion in both men and women, to steal destinies and destroy lives. The manifestations of this evil spirit appeal to the flesh so cunningly, that few have been able to resist her allure ....#000615 $11.95

GOING HOME—*Gwen Shaw.* This book is a treasure which answers so many questions and comforts so many hearts. It gives strength and faith, and helps one to cope with the pain of the loss of a loved one. This book is not really a book about dying, but about *Going Home* to our Eternal Abode with our loving Heavenly Father ....#000607 $8.00 • #000607 *Sale..4 for $20*

KEEPING GOD'S SECRETS—*Gwen Shaw.* This classic teaching on learning to keep God's secrets will help you discern many difficult situations you may face in the coming days.............. #000609 $7.00

LOVE, THE LAW OF THE ANGELS—*Gwen Shaw.* Undoubtedly the greatest of Gwen Shaw's writings, it carries a message of healing and life in a sad and fallen world. Love heals the broken-hearted and sets disarray in order. You will never be the same after reading this beautiful book about love ....#000601 $10.00 ...... • Spanish #000601SP $10.00 • French #000601FR $10.00

SIGI AND I — *Gwen Shaw.* An international best-seller in the 1970's, this exciting story about Sister Gwen's adventures smuggling Bibles behind the Iron Curtain with her co-worker Sigi will grip your heart with excitement. Be filled with courage to go beyond your fears and obey God..........................#000907 $6.50

SONG OF LOVE—*Gwen Shaw*. She was a heart-broken missionary, far from home. She cried out to God for help. He spoke, "Turn to the Song of Solomon and read!" As she turned in obedience, the Lord took her into the "Throne Room" of Heaven and taught her about the love of Christ for His Bride, the church. She fell in love with Jesus afresh, and you will too .... #000401 $7.50
.... • French #000401FR $7.50

SWORD OF LOVE — *Gwen Shaw*. Pakistan is playing a very important role in today's news, and many do not know the true history of that nation. Sis. Gwen was there during the war in 1971 with Sigi. They preached to the parents of today's Taliban. They saw God do miracles, signs and wonders among the people whose sons we are fighting today. Get a vision for Pakistan!
.... #000906 $11.00

THE FALSE FAST — *Gwen Shaw*. Now, from the pen of Gwen Shaw, author of *Your Appointment With God* (a Bible Study on fasting), comes an exposé on the False Fast. It will help you to examine your motives for fasting, and make your foundations sure, so that your fast will be a potent tool in the hands of God
.... #000602 $2.50

THE LIGHT WILL COME FROM RUSSIA — *Gwen Shaw*. The thrilling testimony of Mother Barbara, Abbess of the convent on Mount of Olives. She shares prophecies given her concerning the nations of the world by a holy bishop of the Kremlin, just prior to the Russian Revolution .... #000606 $5.50

THE PARABLE OF THE GOLDEN RAIN—*Gwen Shaw*. This is the story of how revivals come and go, and a true picture, in parable language, of how the Church tries to replace the genuine move of the Spirit with man-made programs and tactics. It's amusing and convicting at the same time .... #000603 $4.00

THEY SHALL MOUNT UP WITH WINGS AS EAGLES — *Gwen Shaw.* Though you may feel old or tired, if you wait on the Lord, you shall mount up on wings as eagles! Let this book encourage you to stretch your wings and fulfill your destiny—no matter what your age!...#000604 $6.95
....• French #000604FR $6.95

TO BE LIKE JESUS — *Gwen Shaw.* Based on her Throne Room experience in 1971, the author shares the Father's heart about our place as sons in His Family. Nothing is more important than *To Be Like Jesus*! .... #000605 $6.95

Women of the Bible Series

In the style of historical novels, Gwen Shaw
opens a window into the lives of the women of the Bible.
Get all 6 books for $27.00 .... #Bible St Women

EVE—MOTHER OF US ALL — *Gwen Shaw.* Read the life story of the first woman. Discover the secrets of one of the most neglected and misunderstood stories in history...................................#000801 $4.50

SARAH—PRINCESS OF ALL MANKIND — *Gwen Shaw.* She was beautiful — and barren. Feel the heartbeat and struggles of this woman who left so great an impact on us all ....#000802 $4.50

REBEKAH—THE BRIDE — *Gwen Shaw.* The destiny of the world was determined when Rebekah said three simple words, "I will go!" Enjoy this touching story of the bride of Isaac............#000803 $4.50

LEAH AND RACHEL—THE TWIN WIVES OF JACOB — *Gwen Shaw.* You will feel their dreams, their pains, their jealousies, their love for one man..#000804 $4.50

MIRIAM—THE PROPHETESS — *Gwen Shaw.* Miriam was the first female to lead worship, the first woman to whom the Lord gave the title "Leader of God's people." ....#000805 $7.50

DEBORAH AND JAEL — *Gwen Shaw.* May God's "warrior women" now arise to take their place in the end-time battle for the harvest! ....#000806 $4.50

In-Depth Bible Studies
(for the Serious Student of God's Word)

FORGIVE AND RECEIVE—*Gwen Shaw.* This Bible Study is a lesson to the church on the much-needed truths of forgiveness and restoration. The epistle to Philemon came from the heart of Paul who had experienced great forgiveness..#000406 $7.00

GRACE ALONE—*Gwen Shaw.* This study teaches the reader to gain freedom in the finished work of the Cross by forsaking works which cannot add to salvation and live by *Grace Alone*..#000402 $13.00

MYSTERY REVEALED — *Gwen Shaw.* Search the depths of God's riches in one of Paul's most profound epistles, "to the praise of His glory!" Learn the "mystery" of the united Body of Christ..........................#000403 $15.00

OUR GLORIOUS HEAD—*Gwen Shaw.* This book teaches vital truths for today, assisting the reader in discerning false teachings, when the philosophies of men are being promoted as being the truths of God. Jesus Christ is the Head of His Body...................#000404 $9.00

THE CATCHING AWAY! —*Gwen Shaw.* This is a very timely Bible Study because Jesus is coming soon! The book of 1 Thessalonians explains God's revelation to Paul on the rapture of the saints. 2 Thessalonians reveals what will happen after the rapture when the antichrist takes over ....#000407 $13.00

THE LOVE LETTER—*Gwen Shaw.* Another of Gwen Shaw's expository Bibles Studies on Paul's Epistles. This study of the letter to the first church of Europe will give the reader an understanding of Paul's great love for the church that was born out of his suffering .... #000405 $9.00

Get the Set of All 6 In-Depth Bible Studies.....#Bible St 6 $53.00

Beloved Bible Study Course

THE TRIBES OF ISRAEL—*Gwen Shaw.* This popular and well-loved study on the thirteen tribes of Israel will show you your place in the spiritual tribes. Understand yourself and others better through this Course ....#000501 $45.00 ....13 CD set - #CTGS1 $50.00

Classic Bible Studies

BEHOLD THE BRIDEGROOM COMETH! —*Gwen Shaw.* A Bible Study on the soon return of Jesus Christ. With so many false teachings these days, it is important that we realize how imminent the rapture of the saints of God really is#000304 $6.50 ....• Italian #000304IT $6.50 .... • Russian #000304RU $0.50

ENDUED WITH LIGHT TO REIGN FOREVER — *Gwen Shaw.* This deeply profound Bible Study reveals the characteristics of the eternal, supernatural, creative light of God as found in His Word. The "Father of Lights," created man in His image. He longs for man to step out of darkness and into His light#000306 $5.00 ....• French #000306FR $8.00

GOD'S END-TIME BATTLE-PLAN—*Gwen Shaw.* This Study on spiritual warfare gives you the biblical weapons for gaining the victory through dancing, shouting, praising, uplifted hands, marching, etc. It has been a great help to many who have been bound by tradition..#000305 $8.00 .... • Spanish #000305SP $5.00 ....• French #000305FR $8.00 ....• Russian #000305RU $.50

IT'S TIME FOR REVIVAL—*Gwen Shaw.* A Bible Study on Revival that not only gives scriptural promises of the end-time revival, but also presents the stories of revivals in the past and the revivalists whom God used. It will stir your heart and encourage you to believe for great revival ....#000311 $7.75

OUR MINISTERING ANGELS—*Gwen Shaw.* A scriptural Bible Study on the topic of angels. Angels will be playing a more and more prominent part in these last days. We need to understand about them and their ministry ....#000308 $8.00 ....• French #000308FR $6.00 ....• Russian #000308RU $8.00

POUR OUT YOUR HEART—*Gwen Shaw.* A wonderful Bible Study on travailing prayer. The hour has come to intercede before the throne of God. The call to intercession is for everyone, and we must carry the Lord's burden and weep for the lost so that the harvest can be brought in quickly . #000301 $5.00
....• Spanish #000301SP $3.00
....• French #000301FR $3.00
.... • Russian #000301RU $8.00
....• Italian #000301IT $6.50
....• Japanese #000301JA $6.50
.... • Chinese #000301CH $

REDEEMING THE LAND—*Gwen Shaw.* This important teaching will help you know your authority through the Blood of Jesus to dislodge evil spirits, break curses, and restore God's blessing upon the land.
....#000309 $9.50
.... • Spanish #000309SP $9.50
....• French #000309FR $9.50
....• Italian #000309IT $9.50

THE FINE LINE—*Gwen Shaw.* This Bible Study clearly magnifies the "fine line" difference between the soul realm and the spirit realm. Both are intangible and therefore cannot be discerned with the five senses, but must be discerned by the Holy Spirit and the Word of God ....#000307 $6.00
....• French #000307FR $10.50

THE POWER OF THE PRECIOUS BLOOD—*Gwen Shaw.* A Bible Study on the Blood of Jesus. The author shares how it was revealed to her how much Satan fears Jesus' Blood. This Bible Study will help you overcome and destroy the works of Satan in your life and the lives of loved ones
....#000303 $5.00
....• Spanish #000303SP $3.00
....• Chinese #000303CH $1.00
....• French #000303FR $3.00
....• Italian #000303IT $5.00
....• Polish #000303PO $0.50
.... • Russian #000303RU $0.50

Get all 12 of these life-changing Bible Studies
....#Bible St. 12 $59.00

THE POWER OF PRAISE—*Gwen Shaw*. When God created the heavens and earth He was surrounded by praise. Miracles happen when holy people praise a Holy God! Praise is the language of creation. If prayer can move the hand of God, how much more can praise move Him! ....#000312 $5.00

YE SHALL RECEIVE POWER FROM ON HIGH *Gwen Shaw*. This is a much needed foundational teaching on the Baptism of the Holy Spirit. It will enable you to teach this subject, as well as to understand these truths more fully yourself .....#000310 $5.00 .... • Spanish #000310SP $3.00• Chinese #000310CH $

YOUR APPOINTMENT WITH GOD—*Gwen Shaw*. A Bible Study on fasting. Fasting is one of the most neglected sources of power over bondages of Satan that God has given the Church. The author's experiences are shared in this Bible Study in a way that will change your life.......................................#000302 $5.00

....• Spanish #000302SP $3.00
....• Chinese #000302CH $3.00
....• French #000302FR $5.00
....• German #000302GE $4.50
....• Italian #000302IT $5.00
....• Japanese #000302JA $3.00
....• Russian #000302RU $1.00

Pocket Sermon Booklets

THE ANOINTING BREAKS THE YOKE —*Gwen Shaw*. Learn how the anointing of God can set you free from your bondage — **free to fulfill your destiny** in the call of God on your life! .....#000710 $2.00 .... • Spanish #000710SP $2.00

BEHOLD, THIS DREAMER COMETH — *Gwen Shaw*. Dreams and dreamers are God's gift to humanity to bring His purposes into the hearts of mankind. This message of the life of Joseph, the dreamer, will encourage you to believe God to fulfill the dream He has put into your heart ....#000707 $2.00 • Spanish #000707SP $2.00

BORN FOR SUCH A TIME AS THIS — *Gwen Shaw.* God is getting His army ready for the greatest battle ever—an army of volunteers; a people totally dedicated, totally surrendered, totally abandoned to the Lord, chosen by the works of God that have already been wrought in their lives................... #000720 $2.50

BREAKTHROUGH — *Gwen Shaw.* If you need a "breakthrough" in your life, this book reveals the truth in a fresh and living way! ....
....000708 $2.00

THE CHANGING OF THE GUARD — Gwen Shaw. This seasoned General in God's army, challenges the next generation to take up the torch and "do or die" in following the call of God. You will be challenged to give up all for the cause of Christ ... #000719 $2.00

THE CHURCH OF THE OPEN ARMS — *Gwen Shaw.* Sister Gwen had a life-changing dream that has given her a fresh vision for the lost and for loving the unlovely. It is time to answer the call to be "The Church of the Open Arms." ....#000713 $2.00

THE CRUCIFIED LIFE—*Gwen Shaw.* When you suffer, knowing the cause is not your own sin, having searched your heart; then you must accept that it is God doing a new thing in your life. Let joy rise up within you because you are a partaker of Christ's suffering ....
....#000701 $2.00

DON'T STRIKE THE ROCK! — *Gwen Shaw.* Moses first struck the Rock in obedience. When he became angry with the rebellion of the people and disobeyed God's new order to speak to the Rock, it cost him his entrance into the Promised Land. Don't allow anything to keep you from fulfilling God's perfect will for your life!...........#000704 $2.00
....• French #000704FR $2.00

FROM PEAK TO PEAK — *Gwen Shaw.* Mountains are the challenges that God puts in our lives and the peaks are places of destiny that God lays before us. Press in to God to find the courage that only He gives to take you from peak to peak to fulfill His destiny for you..#000718 $2.00

GOD WILL DESTROY THE VEIL OF BLINDNESS *"...as the veil of the Temple was rent...I shall again rend the veil in two....for... the Arab, so they shall know that I am God...."* This is the word of the Lord concerning God's plan for the Moslem nations in the days to come... ....#000712 $2.00

HASTENING OUR REDEMPTION — *Gwen Shaw.* All of Heaven and Earth are waiting for the Body of Christ to rise up in maturity and reclaim what we lost in the Fall of Man. Applying the Blood of Jesus is the key to *Hastening Our Redemption* ....#000705 $2.00

IT CAN BE AVERTED — *Gwen Shaw.* Many people today are burdened and fearful over prophecies of doom and destruction. But the Bible is clear that God prefers mercy over judgment when His people humble themselves and pray ....#000706 $2.00
....• Spanish #000706SP $2.00

IT'S TIME FOR CHANGE—After 911, everyone has agreed that "Things will never be the same!" But thank God! The Almighty is still on the throne, and nothing can happen which He does not permit! .... #000714 $2.00

KAIROS TIME — *Gwen Shaw.* That once in a lifetime golden opportunity is sovereignly given to us by the Almighty. What we do with it can change our lives and possibly even change the world. ....#000709 $2.00
....• Spanish #000709SP $2.00

KNOWING ONE ANOTHER IN THE SPIRIT—*Gwen Shaw.* Find great peace as you learn to understand the difficulties your friends, enemies and loved ones face that help to form their character. "... *henceforth know we no man after the flesh.."* (II Cor. 5:16a)..............
....#000703 $2.00
....• French #000703FR $2.00

THE MASTER IS COME AND CALLETH FOR THEE — *Gwen Shaw.* How the Lord called Gwen Shaw to begin the ministry of the End-Time Handmaidens and Servants. Is the Master also calling you into His service? Bring Him the fragments of your life — He will put them together again......................................#000702 $2.00

THE MERCY SEAT— *Gwen Shaw.* The Days of Grace are coming to a close, and the Days of Mercy are now here. And oh, how we need mercy! There never has been a time when we needed it more!
....#000711 $2.00

TEACH THEM TO WEEP —*Gwen Shaw.* "My people don't know how to pray!" I answered, "How can I teach them to pray?" He said, "It's too late to teach them to pray. But you can teach them to weep."..............
....#000716 $2.00

THAT WE MAY BE ONE —*Gwen Shaw.* Only one thing can unite the children of the Lord: the Glory of God. One of Jesus' last prayers was that all of God's children might be one. His prayer still rings out across the ages and convicts us of our lack of unity!..............#000715 $2.00

THROW THE HEAD OF SHEBA OVER THE WALL! —*Gwen Shaw.* David's enemy led an insurrection against him immediately following Absolom's revolt. A great mother in Israel intervened to put a stop to the uprising and saved her city from destruction. Will you take a stand?..#000717 $2.00

Children's Books

LITTLE ONES TO HIM BELONG—*Gwen Shaw*. Based on the testimonies of children's visions of Heaven and the death of a small Chinese boy, Sister Gwen weaves a delightful story of the precious joys of Heaven for children of all ages...#000901 $9.00

TELL ME THE STORIES OF JESUS—*Gwen Shaw.* Some of the greatest New Testament stories of the Life of Jesus, written in a way that will interest children and help them to love Jesus...#000902 $9.00

Books About Heaven

INTRA MUROS (Within the Gates) unabridged — *Rebecca Springer.* One of the most beautiful books about Heaven. Read the glorious account of this ordinary believer's visit to Heaven. Learn what paradise is like.....................................#109101 $8.00

PARADISE, THE HOLY CITY AND THE GLORY OF THE THRONE — *Elwood Scott.* Visited by a saint of God who spent forty days in Heaven, Elwood Scott's detailed description will edify and comfort your heart. Especially good for those with lost loved ones. Look into Heaven! ....#104201 $8.00

Prophecies and Visions

THE DAY OF THE LORD IS NEAR: Vol. I - IV—*Engeltal Press.* "Surely the Lord GOD will do nothing, but he revealeth his secret unto his servants the prophets." (Amos 3:7) A collection of prophecies, visions and dreams. This startling compilation will help you understand what God has in His heart for the near future .... Vol. I - IV with binder #001000 $25.00

More Books Published by Engeltal Press

BANISHED FOR FAITH — *Emil Waltner.* The stirring story of the courageous forefathers of Gwen Shaw, the Hutterite Mennonites, who were banished from their homeland and suffered great persecution for their faith. Index and epilogue by Gwen Shaw........... #126201 $12.95

BECOMING A SERVANT — *Robert Baldwin.* Learn what is on God's heart about servanthood. We must learn to serve before we can be trusted to lead. If you want to be great in God's Kingdom, learn to be the servant of all..#006901 $2.00

FIVE STONES AND A SWORD — *Gene Little.* The true account of Jesus appearing to His lost Moslem children, and revealing Himself to these sons of Abraham. Your heart will leap with joy, and you will be encouraged, with new faith, that God will send a great revival to them .... #072501 $2.00

FROM DUST TO GLORY — *June Lewis.* The Lord intends more than just salvation for us. He is making vessels of eternal Glory if we submit to Him. Rise up from your dust!........................#072001 $7.50

HOLY ANN — *Helen Bingham.* This humble Irish woman moved the arm of God through simple faith and prevailing prayer. Read these modern miracles that are told like a story from the Old Testament. The record of a lifetime of answered prayer .... #010501 $4.95

IT WAS WORTH IT ALL — *Elly Matz.* The story of a beautiful woman whose courage will inspire you. Feel her heart as she tells of her starving father, the young Communist engineer she married, the villages mysteriously evacuated, the invading German army, the concentration camp where she was a prisoner, and her escape into freedom...#078001 $5.95

LET'S KEEP MOVING — *Pete Snyder.* Travel with Peter to Haiti where he struggles with the call of God to be a missionary. Identify with Peter's growth of faith through trials and tribulations as he travels on to China where new adventures await and faithful endurance is needed. A must for the called! ....#108801 $9.95

RULING IN THEIR MIDST — *June Lewis.* The Lord has called us to rule even in the midst of all demonic activity and Satan's plans and schemes. Sister June has learned spiritual warfare from the Lord Himself, "who teacheth my hands to war," in the face of personal tragedy ....#072002 $6.00 • Spanish #072002SP $5.50

VOYAGE TO DOOM — *Arthur D. Morse.* The true account of 930 Jews who boarded the *S.S. St. Louis*, believing they were bound for a safe haven in Cuba, only to find out they had been deceived. This heart-wrenching story will reveal to you the blood that is on the hands of the nations who refused to accept "the least of these my brethren."
....#083001 $2.00

Give a gift certificate from the End-Time Handmaidens Bookstore!

Prices are subject to change.
For a complete catalogue with current pricing, contact:

Engeltal Press
P.O. Box 447 • Jasper, ARK 72641 U.S.A.
Telephone (870) 446-2665 • Fax (870) 446-2259
Email books@eth-s.org
Website www.engeltalpress.com